WAR IN

War in the Gates

Case Histories from the Book of Judges

John F. Parkinson

JOHN RITCHIE LTD
CHRISTIAN PUBLICATIONS

40 Beansburn, Kilmarnock, Scotland

ISBN-13: 978 1 907731 64 8

Copyright © 2012 by John Ritchie Ltd.
40 Beansburn, Kilmarnock, Scotland

www.ritchiechristianmedia.co.uk

Cover design by Geraint Evans

Typeset by John Ritchie Ltd., Kilmarnock
Printed by Bell & Bain Ltd., Glasgow

**"They chose new gods;
Then there was war in the gates"**

From the *Song of Deborah*, Judges 5:8-9

All Scripture taken from the New King James Version
unless noted otherwise

ABBREVIATIONS

NKJV New King James Version, 1982

KJV   King James Version / Authorised Version, 1611

ESV   Englislh Standard Version, 2001

Contents

Introduction

Has the book of Judges anything to say to people of the twenty-first century? Remarkably, the ancient Canaanite worldview has made a striking comeback in our times. The New Age movement draws heavily from the occult and from pantheistic earth-based religions. Many in the western world are returning to pagan nature worship. The names of Baal and Ashtoreth have simply been replaced with Gaia and mother earth. Western society is abandoning a Christian worldview in exchange for New Age beliefs, Postmodernism, Secularism and the New Atheism. Like the Israelites in the times of the Judges, they have chosen new gods - a choice which will bring heavy consequences. The book of Judges has much to say to our twenty-first century pluralistic world.

For the Christian, the book has inestimable value. The inspired writer to the Hebrews, when compiling that great gallery of faith in Chapter 11, included four of the judges by name, *"For time would fail me to tell of Gideon, Barak, Samson, Jephthah... who through faith conquered kingdoms, worked righteousness,obtained promises, stopped the mouths of lions, quenched the violence of fire, escaped the edge of the sword, out of weakness were made strong, became valiant in battle, turned to flight the armies of the aliens"* (Heb 11:32-34). Quite apart from any other considerations, this high commendation ought to be sufficient incentive to read and reread the book of Judges.

The literary genre of the book of Judges is the short story. Christians do not read the Bible for literary reasons alone; nevertheless, we should be aware of the rich treasure-store of literature that comprises the inspired volume. Even secular writers have acknowledged that the book of Judges is one of the greatest collections of short stories in the whole world of literature. From a purely literary point of view, the stories are compelling and fascinating. Some are inspiring, while others are tragic. It is vital that we read them all.

Yet we read the book of Judges for a better reason than its literary value, impressive though that may be. We read it because it is the living word of God which speaks to us in real time. The book is historical narrative rather than doctrine, experience rather than theory. This commentary is not written as a verse by verse exposition, but rather a narrative outline. We shall consider the book story by story, and judge by judge.

The stories are set in the time when Israel was a theocracy, beginning with the death of Joshua and ending just before Samuel's appearance as a national leader. The period covered is about three hundred and thirty years, from 1425–1095 B.C. Nothing is known about the authorship. The book is a compilation, and possibly did not arrive at its present form until centuries after the events described. For example, there is a reference to the Assyrian captivity (18:30). The book ends with the reflection that "In those days there was no king in Israel" (21:25), which would seem to indicate that it was written and compiled at some time during the monarchy.

As we read through the book, we will learn about the nature of humanity, and God's patience and grace. We shall observe the repeating cyclical pattern of unfaithfulness, oppression, repentance and deliverance. We shall discover that the Lord's people had many enemies who wanted to bring them back into slavery. We shall also learn that God was merciful and faithful in that He raised up judges to deliver the people from their oppressors. In a small way, these judges foreshadowed the One who would later come into the world to save us from a tyranny worse than any Canaanite could impose.

The enemies of the Israelites could quite literally be identified as 'flesh and blood', real people to be destroyed on actual battlefields. The enemies included Mesopotamians, Moabites,

Canaanites, Midianites, Amalekites, Ammonites, and Philistines. However, the Christian's struggle today is not with 'flesh and blood' people on literal battlefields, but with principalities, powers, world rulers of this present darkness, and spiritual hosts of wickedness in heavenly places. God used Israel as an instrument of judgement on the indigenous peoples of Canaan. God had long endured the rebellion and sin of the inhabitants, until the iniquity of the Amorites was complete (Gen 15:16). In His sovereign right and wisdom, God judged the people of the land, giving the onerous work to the nation of Israel. The church of this age, by contrast, has been given no such task. Quite the opposite. Paul exhorted the believers in Rome to, "Bless those who persecute you; bless and do not curse" (Rom 12:14). The characteristic truth of Christianity is not judgement, but grace. It is not for Christians to slay unbelievers on a battlefield, but to preach the gospel to the whole creation (Mk 16:15).

A significant change for the worse takes place during the course of the book. Up to the time of Gideon, the people of Israel were slaying their Gentile enemies. From Gideon onward, they were slaying their own Hebrew brethren. This is a very salutary lesson for saints today. It is profoundly sad when Christians misdirect their energy by attacking one another, instead of taking the fight into enemy territory by the preaching of the gospel.

The stories of Judges contain vital lessons for individual believers, for local churches, and for national governments. The book stands as a divine warning to all ages about the moral chaos which results when men choose darkness rather than light. The Israelites of three thousand years ago turned their backs on the God of Abraham, Isaac and Jacob, and embraced the gods of Canaanite imagination. In parallel, today's postmodern world is rejecting the eternal and absolute truths of scripture in favour of relativism and pluralism, yet our own society carries far more responsibility and guilt than the ancient Israelites. Why should that be? Because "light has come into

11

the world, and men loved darkness rather than light" (John 3:19). Nevertheless, we see in the book of Judges individual examples of men and women living by faith in an ungodly environment. And these judges were simply imperfect examples and foreshadows of the Son of God who came into the world to save sinners. Let us heed the warnings of Judges and draw nearer to the true and living God. May God be pleased to use this book to help our understanding of His word and to strengthen our faith.

John F. Parkinson
N. Ireland
2012

CHAPTER ONE

Judges 1:1 – 3:11

Othniel against the Mesopotamians

Eight years of miserable enslavement by a cruel invader was as much as the people of Israel could endure. In their desperation, they cried to the LORD for deliverance. It was a strange irony for the descendants of Abraham to be subjugated by Mesopotamians. About 400 years earlier, in Mesopotamia, the God of glory had appeared to Abraham and said to him:

> "Get out of your country,
> From you family
> And from your father's house,
> To a land that I will show you.
> I will make you a great nation;
> I will bless you
> And make your name great;
> And you shall be a blessing.
> I will bless those who bless you,
> And I will curse him that curses you;
> And in you all the families of the earth shall be blessed."

(Gen 12:1-3).

Abraham's life was changed from that defining moment. He had seen the LORD. How difficult it must have been for one of Abraham's Mesopotamian neighbours to make sense of his decision to leave Ur of the Chaldees. Such a fine city seemed to be the ideal place to bring up one's family. There was an abundance of art and culture, commerce and trade, law and order. And of course there was religion with its strong esoteric and sensual appeal. Without doubt, Mesopotamia was the place of opportunity. An ambitious man could develop a career in business, trade, agriculture or priesthood. Today's museums abound with spectacular and beautiful examples of Mesopotamian art and craftsmanship. It is not without good reason that the region has been called the cradle of civilisation.

Should Abraham's Mesopotamian neighbour have asked him where he was intending to resettle upon leaving Ur, he would not have received an intelligible answer. The truth was that Abraham himself did not know where he was going. The writer to the Hebrews informs us that "he went out, not knowing where he was going" (Heb 11:8). The critical point was that Mesopotamia, with all its attractions, had lost its appeal for Abraham. His eyes had seen a sight that infinitely surpassed the glory of Ur – he had seen the LORD, the God of glory. He was looking for "a city which has foundations, whose builder and maker is God" (Heb 11:10). He had believed God and had moved out in faith. He had finished with Mesopotamia. As Christians reading the book of Judges, we can discern that *Mesopotamia is a powerful symbol of friendship with the world, a love of everything that this world has to offer.*

Four centuries after Abraham had forsaken Ur, his descendants were in the promised land, but in slavery to King Cushan-rishathaim of Mesopotamia whose name meant 'Cushan of double-wickedness'. As a redeemed people, Israel's days of slavery ought to have been over forever, but now we find them humiliated and crying to the LORD for deliverance. What had gone wrong?

Life after Joshua

The death of a great statesman sometimes signals the passing of an era and heralds the dawn of a new age in the life of a nation. An outstanding leader will often shape the character and aspirations of the people, setting an example and plotting a clear course for them to follow. When such a leader dies, the nation must make its choice whether to continue in the same course or to change direction. When Moses died, God had another servant by the name of Joshua, ready to lead the people with the same vision and faithfulness that Moses had shown. It is no exaggeration to say that Joshua proved to be one of the greatest national leaders of all time. We read, "On that day the LORD exalted Joshua in the sight of all Israel; and they feared him, as they had feared Moses, all the days of his life" (Josh 4:14). Joshua's death (c.1380 B.C.) was the end of an era, and the beginning of a new epoch in the life of Israel which continued through to the time of Samuel the prophet.

Joshua, described as "the servant of the LORD", died at the age of 110 years and was buried in his own inheritance in the hill country of Ephraim. He had finished his course well, having led the people of Israel into the land of promise, and having appointed each tribe to its God given inheritance. It was after his death that the people had inquired of the LORD as to who should lead the assault against the Canaanites. Judah, after conquering the Canaanites, went on to possess Jerusalem and Hebron, the hill country, the lowlands, and the desert region of Negeb. Their conquests also included Zephath, Gaza and Ashkelon. For a time, Judah was enjoying spectacular victories under God. The future seemed bright and glorious.

The book of Judges begins with the people of Israel in the promised land, inquiring of the Lord for guidance, an excellent start by any standard. The people had prayed, "Who shall be first to go up for us against the Canaanites to fight against them?" (1:1). The LORD's answer was swift and clear - the tribe of Judah was to lead the assault. In a commendable display of solidarity, Judah and Simeon united to wage a joint campaign against the Canaanites and Perizites, defeating ten thousand of them at the battle of Bezek. The defeated King Adoni-bezek, whose thumbs and great toes were cut off, willingly acknowledged that he was receiving at God's hand what he had done to at least seventy other kings.

The words of Joshua were still ringing in the ears of the people as victory followed victory, "Now therefore, fear the LORD, serve him in sincerity and in truth; and put away the gods which

15

your fathers served on the other side of the River, and in Egypt. Serve the LORD!" (Josh 24:14). Joshua had challenged the people either to serve the LORD or to choose between the gods beyond the River and the gods of the Amorites. Joshua made his own choice very clear, "...as for me and my house, we will serve the LORD" (Josh 24:15). The people insisted to Joshua that they too would serve the LORD.

In addition to Judah and Simeon, other tribes had also taken possession of their inheritance, but they were not always successful in achieving conclusive victories. We are informed that the tribes of Benjamin, Manasseh, Ephraim, Zebulun, Asher, Naphtali, and Dan were unable to dispel completely the original inhabitants. Even Judah, who had taken the hill country, could not drive out the people of the plain because of their superior military hardware. The inhabitants had chariots of iron, putting Judah at a crippling disadvantage (1:19).

These circumstances, however, were not random or chance events but were part of God's strategic purposes in disciplining and shaping the people of Israel to be a holy and separated people unto Himself. God's words are recorded, "Because this nation has transgressed my covenant which I commanded their fathers, and has not heeded My voice, I also will no longer drive out before them any of the nations which Joshua left when he died, *so through them I may test Israel*, whether they will keep the ways of the LORD, to walk in them as their fathers kept them, or not" (2:20-22). Therefore we read, "the LORD left those nations, without driving them out immediately; nor did he deliver them into the hand of Joshua."

The Christian of this age should have no difficulty in relating to this situation. It has often been asked why God did not complete His work in us the moment we trusted Christ. Of course the believer is complete in Christ in the positional and eternal sense from the moment of conversion, but he is still capable of sinning and does not experience sinless perfection in this life. In other words, the Christian is still living in territory from which the enemy has not been removed. The world, the flesh and the devil are the inveterate enemies of the believer until his last day on earth. And yet such things are allowed by God with the strategic purpose of building up Christian character in the saints. God supplies all the resources that we need to withstand the wiles of the devil. Paul tells us that when the Christian puts on the whole armour of God, he is able to stand in the evil day (Eph 6:10-20). God enables us to live a victorious Christian life right here among our enemies, in the same body in which we were once enslaved to sin. What an incentive and what an encouragement!

Unfortunately, not only did the people of Israel fail to drive out the original inhabitants of the land, but in the course of time they actually imbibed their false world view. Forgetting that they were a redeemed people who belonged to the LORD, they switched their allegiance and devotion to the pagan deities of Canaan. They had forsaken the living and true God for gods of wood and stone. And sadly, it had all happened within one generation from Joshua.

We read that when all of Joshua's generation had died, "another generation arose after them, who did not know the LORD nor the work which he had done for Israel" (2:10). There seemed to be an attraction in idolatry that the Israelites found irresistible. Canaanites worshipped the fertility-god Baal. When Baals are spoken of in the plural, it is the fertility-gods of the different cities or communities that are meant – the same one fertility-god, localised and appropriated by the addition of city names. Israel forsook the LORD, and served Baal.

The female deity of the Canaanites was Astarte or Ashtoreth. Astarte, the equivalent of Ishtar from the Assyro-Babylonian cycle of gods, was identified with the moon and wore the sign of the crescent.[1] The worship of Ashtoreth was associated with groves of trees, whether of artificial planting, or of nature's own providing in wooded valley or hillside.[2] These groves were places of immorality in which the Canaanite worshippers of Baal and Ashtoreth practised sexual fertility rights and human sacrifice. Of all the idolatry of the ancient world, the Canaanite religion ranks as probably the most depraved and cruel. And yet it was to Canaanite Baal worship that the people of Israel would turn again and again in their unfaithfulness and disobedience.

The world view of the Canaanite was typical of any polytheistic earth-based religion. There was a pantheon of gods and goddesses who ruled in the sky, sea, earth and underworld. There were gods of harvest, fertility and war. The Canaanite life view could be reduced to this core belief - *if things were going well for a man, it meant that the gods were pleased; but if things were going badly, the gods were angry.* Therefore the chief aim of a man's religious devotions was to placate and manipulate the gods.[3] Such a belief system was loveless, producing fear and superstition. In the case of the Canaanites, their slavish beliefs had led them to sacrifice their own children alive in the fires of Chemosh and Molech, the Moabite and Ammonite versions of Baal.

What a downward step for the Israelite to forsake the living and true God for the hideous monster of Baal. God had shown His abhorrence of idolatry by issuing an absolute prohibition: "You shall have no other gods before me. You shall not make for yourself a carved image - any likeness of anything that is in heaven above, or that is in the earth beneath, or that is in the water under the earth; you shall not bow down to them or serve them..." (Ex 20:3-5). The Israelites didn't completely forsake God but rather added the false to the true in an early example of religious syncretism. Their belief in the God of Abraham, Isaac and Jacob was hopelessly compromised by their practice of Baal worship.

Plunder and distress

The angel of the LORD delivered the damning indictment to the people at Bochim, "I led you up from Egypt and brought you to the land of which I swore to your fathers; and I said 'I will never break My covenant with you. And you shall make no covenant with the inhabitants of this land; *you shall tear down their altars.'* But you have not obeyed My voice. Why have you done this?'" (2:1-2).

We read how the people of Israel had provoked the LORD to anger by bowing down to the gods of the people, "They forsook the LORD and served Baal and the Ashtoreths" (2:13). The result of this appalling unfaithfulness was to be plundered at the hands of their surrounding enemies. Each time the people were in distress, the LORD would raise up a judge to deliver them from their oppressors. But each time a judge died, the people "reverted and behaved more corruptly than their fathers, by following other gods, to serve them and bow down to them..."(2:19). This cyclical pattern developed into a relentless downward spiral throughout the period of the Judges.

As we have already observed, the first case study of oppression and deliverance in the book of Judges concerns Mesopotamians from the region of Haran. Sadly, the clock had turned back since the days of Abraham. However, God had His judge and deliverer in the right place at the right time. Enter Othniel.

Othniel the deliverer

The flow of history in the book of Judges is not arbitrary. The choices and actions of a society have very definite consequences. Three charges are levelled against Israel (3:7), relating to their deeds, thoughts and affections. Firstly, their deeds are described as evil in the sight of the LORD; secondly, in their thoughts they had forgotten the LORD their God; thirdly, they had turned their affections to the Baals and Ashtoreths of the original inhabitants. They had abandoned the teaching and example of Joshua, and had become evil, faithless and idolatrous. Little wonder we read that God's anger was hot, kindled against Israel. God sold the people into the hand of the doubly-wicked King Cushan-Rishathaim of Mesopotamia. After eight years of servitude the people cried to God for deliverance, and God answered their prayer by raising a deliverer called Othniel.

Othniel had the great privilege in life of having an uncle who was a true believer. Only God can measure the influence that one person may have on other family members. We could think of the influence that Andrew had on his brother Peter when he brought him to Christ, or of the impressions made by a godly mother and grandmother on a young child named Timothy. To have believing parents is a blessing beyond estimate. A Christian can be a great influence on immediate family members and also on those of the extended family. Do we pray for our nephews, nieces and cousins, as well as the immediate members of our own family?

Caleb and Joshua were the only two men who, having come out of Egypt under Moses, had survived to enter Canaan under Joshua. They were two of the original twelve spies that Moses had sent to report back on the land of Canaan. Representatives from each tribe had been chosen to go on the covert mission to spy out the land. Included among the twelve were, "from the tribe of Judah, Caleb the son of Jephunneh" and "from the tribe of Ephraim, Hoshea (Joshua) the son of Nun" (Num 13:6,8). Ten of the spies brought back an evil report of the land, discouraging the people with stories of large fortified cities, giants, innumerable enemies and obstacles. Joshua and Caleb, on the other hand, urged the people to go in and take the land, confident that the LORD would be with them. Consequently God decreed that none of the adult population of that generation, save Joshua and Caleb, would enter Canaan. Only the little ones would survive to enter. God honoured His word to Joshua and Caleb by bringing them into the land, along with those who had been infants at the time of the spies, among whom was a boy named Kenaz, the younger brother of Caleb and future father of Othniel.

Leaving aside the positive family influences that helped to prepare Othniel for his life's work, we also learn that Othniel was chosen by the LORD for this ministry, "The LORD raised up a deliverer for the children of Israel, who delivered them: Othniel the son of Kenaz, Caleb's younger brother" (3:9). He was neither self-appointed nor democratically elected. We read that the Spirit of the LORD came upon him and he judged Israel. There is no greater joy in life than to be in the centre of God's will, knowing for sure that we are being led by the Spirit.

We are not given any details of the decisive battle with the Mesopotamians, save to say, "He went out to war, and the LORD delivered Cushan-Rishathaim king of Mesopotamia into his hand; and his hand prevailed over Cushan-Rishathaim" (3:10). This much we do know, that the outcome of the war was the end of the military dominance of Mesopotamia in Israel. At last the nation had peace, security and righteous rule. In the words of scripture, "the land had rest for forty years" (3:11).

Othniel's helper

There was yet another factor in Othniel's success which is most instructive. Othniel had a spiritual wife who desired her husband's blessing. We read in the first chapter that Caleb had offered his daughter in marriage to the man who would attack Kiriath-sepher and take it. When Othniel attacked the town and took it, Caleb gave his daughter Achsah to him in marriage. Othniel could not have asked for a better wife.

Achsah had the long-term spiritual interests of her husband at heart. She encouraged her husband to increase his inheritance by asking for a field. She also had the foresight to ask for springs of water, knowing that their land was in the dry region of the Negeb. Fully realising the importance of a future water supply, she used her influence with her father to obtain two water sources. We read that her father Caleb gave her the upper springs and the lower springs (1:11-16). Achsah encouraged and helped her husband in enlarging and improving his inheritance. But this is hardly surprising, considering the example that her father had been to her. After all, Achsah was the daughter of Caleb, the man who had boldly pleaded with Joshua, "Give me this mountain..." (Josh 14:12).

It is a good thing when a man finds a wife who is interested in her husband's progress in the things of God. A wife can make or break a man in Christian service. We shall see presently how Samson's downfall was his heathen wives. Othniel's success was in great measure due to a supportive wife. The practical implications for us today are obvious. When a Christian, male or female, is looking for a life partner, they do well to make sure that they share a common interest in spiritual things, and that they will be a blessing to one another and to others.

God had raised a deliverer who saved his people from their oppressors and who gave Israel peace for forty years. In the first of the short stories, however, there must of necessity be a sad sequel. We read, "Then Othniel the son of Kenaz died" (3:11). Indeed, all the judges in our study will necessarily die.

The Christian, by contrast, can give thanks for a greater than Othniel, our Lord Jesus Christ, who came down from heaven to save His people from a worse oppressor than the Mesopotamians - He came to save us from our sins. He accomplished that mighty deliverance on the cross. But the greatest story of all doesn't end with the fact of His death - there is a glorious sequel! The Lord Jesus rose from the dead, conquering forever the great enemy of death. The deliverance gained by Othniel lasted for forty years, but the deliverance secured by Christ is eternal. Interestingly, Othniel, the first of the judges, was of the tribe of Judah. The Lord Jesus was also born into the tribe of Judah, one of His great titles being "the Lion of the tribe of Judah" (Rev 5:5). It is good to know the heavenly Othniel!

We have suggested that Mesopotamia speaks of *friendship with the world.* John commands us, "Love not the world, neither the things that are in the world. If anyone loves the world, the love of the Father is not in him" (1 John 2:15). What can preserve us as Christians from being attracted and conquered again by a love of the world, just as the Israelites found themselves once again under Mesopotamians? The answer is surely to have a fresh vision and appreciation of Christ – a vision that will eclipse and outshine anything that this world has to offer. "For whatever is born of God overcomes the world. And this is the victory that overcomes the world - our faith. Who is he who overcomes the world, but he who believes that Jesus is the Son of God?" (1 John 5:4-5). Let us have a daily occupation with the Saviour and grow in our appreciation of Him.

---

[1] The sign of the crescent was subsequently adopted by the religion of Islam, the greatest of the Christian heresies.

[2] From Chapter 4 "The Religion of Canaan" in *Assyria* by Zenaide Ragozin (T. Fisher Unwin, London, 1888).

[3] See "Polytheism at Lystra" p.62 in *No Other Doctrine: The Gospel and the Postmodern World* by the present author John Parkinson (John Ritchie Ltd., Kilmarnock, 2005 and 2010).

CHAPTER TWO

Judges 3:12 –3:31

Ehud against the Moabites

One of the greatest evils to come to light in modern times has been that of international child abuse. Fuelled by the rise of the internet, a massive industry has surfaced based on child pornography. This abuse, however, is not confined to those who want to sexually exploit children for financial gain. Government enquiries and reports have exposed the institutionalised and endemic abuse of children by churches and orphanages in numerous countries. We have reacted with horror and shock as we have learned of priests, nuns and carers abusing children who were entrusted to their care, subjecting them to sexual abuse, physical cruelty, and psychological tyranny.

I mention this unpleasant subject because the worst child abusers of all time were probably the Moabites and the Ammonites. Their worship of Baal was so debased that they sacrificed children alive in the fire. Historians tell us of a hollow metal statue with outstretched hands to receive the child victims who would roll from the red hot hands into the furnace within the idol. The screams of the children were drowned out by the noise and din created by the priests. This was to gain the favour of Chemosh the god of the Moabites, and Molech the god of the Ammonites.

It is hard to imagine anything more unlike God, or indeed anything further removed from the truth about God. The devil had turned man's perception of worship into a grotesque parody of truth. The men of Moab had become utterly perverse in their worship of Baal. There was not a single redeeming feature in the religious beliefs associated with the worship of Chemosh. There was nothing spiritual about Moabitism. Their religion was entirely fleshly, sensual and devilish. *Moab speaks of the flesh, and of fleshly religion at its worst.*

The Hamitic peoples of the Middle East, especially those descended through Canaan and Sidon, practised child sacrifice on a wide scale. The Phoenicians, who came from Tyre, spread the practice to their other settlements. In the ruins of Carthage in North Africa, archaeologists discovered 20,000 terracotta urns containing the cremated remains of infants. Many of the urns are dedicated to Baal, while some have the word *mlk*, standing for Moloch. It is recorded that a Roman legion once came upon a group of Carthaginians while the sacrifice of children was taking place, "The Romans, then the rulers of the world, were not noted for gentleness or tender-heartedness. Yet when a Roman legion under the reign of Tiberius came upon the priests of Molech in the midst of a child sacrifice, so great was their horror and pity that they not only dispersed the crowd and released the victims, as many as were still living, but hung every one of the priests, forbidding the repetition of the unnatural rite in future."[4]

It is difficult for anyone looking at these things from the twenty-first century to understand why the people of Israel were attracted to Baal worship and child sacrifice. The commandment had been given through Moses, " And you shall not let any of your descendants pass through the fire to Molech, nor shall you profane the name of your God: I am the LORD" (Lev 18:21). And yet incredibly, to King Solomon's dishonour, we read, "Then Solomon built a high place for Chemosh the abomination of Moab, on the hill that is east of Jerusalem, and for Molech, the abomination of the people of Ammon" (1 Kings 11:7). Although Solomon himself is not associated with child sacrifice, nevertheless the altars remained a snare to the people until they were destroyed much later by good King Josiah. God condemned the horrendous practice of child sacrifice through the prophet Jeremiah, "And they built the high places of Baal which are in the valley of the son of Hinnom, to cause their sons and their daughters to pass through the fire to Molech; which I did not command them, nor did it come into My mind, that they should do this abomination, to cause Judah to sin" (Jer 32:35). In the ancient world of the Old Testament, the worst offenders of this abomination appear to have been the Moabites and the Ammonites.

Before we sit in judgement on the ancient world, we ought to remember that there is another form of 'child sacrifice' practised today on a scale that would have shocked even the Moabites and the Ammonites.   There are forty-two million abortions worldwide every year.   There are medical reasons in the case of a minority, but about 93% are for social reasons, i.e. the child is unwanted or inconvenient. Sadly, Chemosh and Molech have not gone away.

In Genesis 10 we read how the present earth was populated from the three sons of Noah - Shem, Ham and Japheth. The Moabites and Ammonites were not racially Hamitic. They were actually Semitic, their fathers Moab and Ammon being the sons of Lot by his two daughters. The result of this sordid act of incest was to produce two inveterate enemies of Israel. Although Moab and Ammon were descended from Shem and not Ham, culturally they assimilated the lifestyle of the Hamitic Canaanites. In fact, they seemed happy to push the extremes of religious barbarity beyond that of the other Canaanites.

When Israel was being led through the wilderness toward Canaan, they were warned not to meddle with the Moabites and Ammonites (related to Israel through Lot), nor with the Edomites (related to Israel through Esau). Israel observed this command and did not interfere with their inheritance, yet the three nations denied Israel safe passage or refreshment on their weary desert journey (Deut 2:4-19). The second short story is told against a background of Moabites.

Eglon, King of Moab

When Othniel died, the people of Israel "again did evil in

the sight of the LORD" (3:12). We are not told what the specific evil was, but the lessons learned under Othniel were obviously forgotten. The forty years of peace were not acknowledged as coming from the LORD. The narrator tells us in chilling words, "So the LORD strengthened Eglon king of Moab against Israel" (3:12). Doubtless this was for Israel's long-term good, but the chastening would be bitter and hard. It turned out to be eighteen years of servitude under the Moabite heel.

King Eglon mustered military help from two other enemies of Israel, the Ammonites and Amalekites. We have already thought about the origin and character of the Moabites and the Ammonites. Who then were the Amalekites? Amalek was the grandson of Esau. His mother was called Timna, concubine to Eliphaz, Esau's son (Gen 36:12,16). The crimes of the Amalekites were despicable in the extreme. When the Israelites came out of Egypt, faint and weary from their journey, they were attacked by Amalekites who cut down those who were lagging behind. God gave instructions through Moses that the memory of Amalek should be blotted out under heaven. The prophet Samuel referred to them as "the sinners, the Amalekites" (1 Sam 15:18).

It is something of an understatement to say that Moab, Ammon, and Amalek all had strange and defiled pedigrees. What an army of anti-Israel, God-defying sinners that King Eglon gathered together to defeat Israel! To the shame of Israel, Eglon occupied Jericho, the city of palms, a place forever associated with the victory of God's great servant, Joshua. After eighteen years of servitude, the people of Israel again cried to the LORD.

Ehud and his two edged sword

Just as the LORD had raised up Othniel, so we read, "the LORD raised up a deliverer for them: Ehud the son of Gera, the Benjamite, a left-handed man" (3:15). The action begins with the people of Israel sending tribute by Ehud to King Eglon of Moab. How sad! God's chosen people, in the land that God had promised to Abraham, having to pay tribute to a king of Moab.

Ehud was a fine example of a strategic thinker. He formulated a plan and made timely preparations well in advance of the action. Ehud had been working on a very special project – a sword. Firstly, he made the sword about a cubit in length (that is about 18 inches or 450mm long). This unusual length meant that the weapon was really something between a sword and a dagger. As we shall see, Ehud had a very good reason for wanting the sword to be this exact length. Secondly, it was a two-edged sword. Ehud measured, heated, tempered, hammered, and sharpened the sword to his own specification. There was a lot of hard work involved. It was not the kind of sword one could easily have acquired locally. The narrator tells us that he made it for himself. He knew exactly what he wanted it for.

Ehud was a left-handed man. Such a seemingly insignificant detail might seem irrelevant, but the fact is that the majority of people in Ehud's day, just as in our own day, were right-handed. This meant that if you did not fully trust a man, you would keep a watchful eye on his right hand. Ehud understood this instinctive behaviour very well and took full advantage of it. He assumed that Eglon would be no different from anyone else, and that, through sheer force of habit, would be watching Ehud's right hand. Ehud concealed the sword on his right thigh under his clothes.

The party of Israelites duly delivered the tribute to Eglon and set off on their homeward journey. On reaching the sculptured stones near Gilgal, Ehud instructed the party to continue going. He, however, did not join them as he had a grim job to do on behalf of his people. He turned his horse around and returned to the king. On arriving at the house, Ehud announced that he had a secret message for the king. The king duly dismissed all his attendants, and Ehud entered the cool roof chamber where Eglon was sitting. The two men were now alone in the room. The time had come to put his plan into action. The many hours of preparation were about to prove invaluable.

It can safely be assumed that no one, especially a representative of a subject race, was ever allowed to enter the presence of the king carrying arms. All weapons, if they were carried for protection on the journey, would doubtless be removed before entering the royal household. No one suspected that day that Ehud was carrying a sword. It was expertly concealed under his clothes on his right thigh. There were no body searches and no security checks.

"I have a message from God for you" said Ehud to Eglon. The narrator informs us that Eglon was a very fat man. He began to rise from his seat. This was the moment when he would be slightly off balance, moving in slow cumbersome fashion as is the manner of very heavy people. Eglon was now at his most vulnerable.

Eglon would hardly have known what hit him. In a flash, with his left hand Ehud drew the sword from his right thigh, and thrust it into the fat belly of king Eglon. The king was so obese that the sword disappeared in the fat. The narrator then adds in stomach-churning detail, "and the dirt came out" (3:22 KJV). With the presence of mind worthy of any special commando, Ehud left the roof chamber, locked the doors behind him, and made a hasty escape. Riding furiously, he passed the sculptured stones and arrived in the safe town of Seirah.

The trumpet sound was soon echoing across the hills of Ephraim, rallying the people to follow Ehud. At last the people of Israel had a leader and deliverer who could defeat the Moabites. God had heard their cry and had granted victory through Ehud. Ehud exhorted the people, "Follow me; for the LORD has delivered your enemies the Moabites into your hand" (3:28).

Meanwhile, Eglon's servants were becoming more and more anxious. Why had Eglon taken so long to appear? On discovering that the doors were locked, they thought that their master was probably relieving himself in the closet. They waited and waited, until eventually they concluded that something was seriously wrong. They inserted the key and unlocked the doors, only to see the dead body of their king lying on the floor. Their long delay in entering the room had given Ehud all the time he needed to escape well clear of the house.

While the Moabites were still suffering from shock, Ehud was proving himself to be an able military strategist by leading his new army to the fords of Jordan. This was good thinking on Ehud's part. Gilgal and the city of palms were west of the river Jordan, while the Moabite home country lay on the eastern side of Jordan. Ehud fully realised that the Moabites, garrisoned near Gilgal, would attempt to make their escape homeward by crossing the river at the shallow fords. Ehud swiftly seized the fords from the Moabites and would not allow any to pass over. The Israelites killed about ten thousand Moabites, all strong able-bodied men. Moab was soundly defeated and was finished as an occupying force. The victory for the Israelites was so overwhelming that "the land had rest for eighty years" (3:30).

King Eglon is a striking picture of the flesh – outwardly pompous and inwardly impure. He was an excessively fat man who lived for eating, drinking and self-indulgence. His god was his belly. This would remind us of Paul's warning to the Philippians that there were those who lived as enemies of the cross of Christ, "whose end is destruction, whose god is their belly, and whose glory is in their shame – who set their minds on earthly things" (Phil 3:19).

There is nothing as barren as flesh-energised religion. The Apostle Paul could recall the time when, as Saul of Tarsus, he put his confidence in the flesh: "If anyone else thinks he may have confidence in the flesh, I more so" (Phil 3:4). Paul gives a long list of the types of things he had once trusted in: his circumcision (on the eighth day); his race (Israel); his tribe (Benjamin); his pedigree (pure Hebrew); his law-keeping (Pharisee); his zeal (persecutor of the church); his righteousness (blameless). How did Paul now regard those things that he formerly depended on? We are left in no doubt as to Paul's convictions, "But what things were gain to me, these I have counted loss for Christ. Yet indeed I also count all things loss for the excellence of the knowledge of Christ Jesus my Lord..." (Phil 3:7-8).

When Ehud thrust the sword into Eglon the 'dirt' came out. What an apt description of the flesh - *dirt*. Paul described the works of the flesh as, "adultery, fornication, uncleanness, lewdness, idolatry, sorcery, hatred, contentions, jealousies, outbursts of wrath, selfish ambitions, dissensions, heresies, envy, murders,drunkenness, revelries, and the like" (Gal 5:19-21). The New Testament portrays the flesh and the Spirit in constant tension and opposition. Paul exhorted the Galatian believers to walk by the Spirit, and not to gratify the desires of the flesh. In contrast to the works of the flesh, Paul tells us that the "fruit of the Spirit is love, joy, peace, longsuffering, kindness, goodness, faithfulness, gentleness, self-control" (Gal 5:22-23). Happily, the believer is empowered to live a life of victory over the flesh, "those who are Christ's have crucified the flesh with its passions and desires."

Ehud has set us a fine example in the area of foresight and preparation. He invested much thought, time and energy in preparing his sword. The success of his mission depended in great measure on the suitability, sharpness, and efficiency of that weapon. Ehud had planned how he would conceal the sword and how he would put it swiftly and accurately to its deadly purpose. There is also a sword which is even sharper than that of Ehud's: "For the word of God is living and powerful, and sharper than any two-edged sword, piercing even to the division of soul and spirit, and of joints and marrow, and is a discerner of the thoughts and intents of the heart" (Heb 4:12). This teaches us that the application of the word of God to ourselves will help us to discern and judge the flesh within us.

The metaphor of the 'sword' as the word of God is again employed by Paul in his great exhortation to put on the armour of God, "And take...the sword of the Spirit, which is the word of God" (Eph 6:17). Do we spend as much time reading and thinking on the Bible, as Ehud did with his literal sword? The importance of constant, prayerful, thoughtful reading of the word of God cannot be overrated.

We have also the supreme example of the Lord Jesus who often challenged His hearers with questions such as, "Have you never read in the scriptures?" (Mat 21:42) During the temptation in the wilderness, the Lord answered Satan three times with Scripture, beginning each time with the weighty and authoritative words, "It is written..." May we have a fresh appreciation of the power and authority of the word of God. Let us be like Ehud and invest much time sharpening the sword so that we will be able, by the Spirit, to judge the flesh and defend the faith.

[4] From Chapter 4 "The Religion of Canaan" in *Assyria* by Zenaide Ragozin (T. Fisher Unwin, London, 1888).

CHAPTER THREE

Judges 3:31

Shamgar against the Philistines

Compared to most of the other judges, Shamgar is a fairly minor player. One verse is sufficient to cover his contribution, and yet it has pleased God to include his name among the more gallant heroes of faith. Perhaps that is the main lesson of this mini case study. Anything done for the Lord will be acknowledged by the Lord.

The Bible is full of surprises. For example, in the list of David's mighty men, the name of Joab is missing while his armour bearer is named among the greats, "Naharai the Beerothite (armourbearer of Joab the son of Zeruiah)" (2 Sam 23:37). Again, we are surprised to read that the poor widow who gave two mites into the treasury had given more than all the rich people. The Lord Jesus made an illuminating value judgement to His disciples about the incident, "Assuredly, I say to you that this poor widow has put in more than all those who have given to the treasury; for they all put in out of their abundance, but she out of her poverty put in all that she had, her whole livelihood" (Mk 12:43-44). Perhaps that is what it will be like at the Judgement Seat of Christ. Many Christians who have had much prominence and praise in this life will have minor recognition then, while countless unsung heroes and heroines of faith will be acclaimed by the Lord on that day. Such is the case of Shamgar.

There is only one other mention of Shamgar in the book of Judges (5:6). The Song of Deborah laments the pitiful conditions in Israel,

> *"In the days of Shamgar, son of Anath,*
> *In the days of Jael,*
> *The highways were deserted*
> *And the travellers walked along the byways.*

The people of Israel were demoralised and humiliated by the people of the land, so much so that they could not even travel on the main thoroughfares for fear of assault. And yet there appears to have been one notable exception – Shamgar, the son of Anath.

The book of Judges informs us that five lords of the Philistines had been left in Canaan along with other original inhabitants in order to prove Israel (3:3). This is the first mention of Philistines in the book. The second mention is to tell us that Shamgar had slain six hundred Philistines with an ox goad (3:31). So who were the Philistines?

The Philistines were descended from Casluhim, the son of Mizraim (Egypt), the son of Ham (Gen 10:14). By the time the people of Israel came out of Egypt, the Hamitic Philistines had settled along the coastal strip from Egypt to Gaza. Five cities are linked with the five lords: Gaza, Ashkelon, Ashdod, Ekron and Gath. The modern name of Palestine is derived from the ancient name of Philistia.

In religious life, the Philistines had their own localised version of Baal worship. Three gods were associated with their beliefs: Dagon (the fish god), Baalzebub (lord of flies), and Ashtoreth. In the Bible, the Philistines are known as the "uncircumcised" Philistines, emphasising their exclusion from the fellowship and promises of God's covenant people. *The Philistines speak of human religion in its uncleanness and alienation from God.* We shall meet the Philistines again in the more extended story of Samson.

In the New Testament the Pharisees accused the Lord Jesus of being empowered by the Philistine demon Beelzebul, "This fellow does not cast out demons except by Beelzebul, the ruler of the demons" (Mt 12:24-28). The Lord responded to this shocking charge by solomnly warning about the unpardonable sin of blasphemy against the Holy Spirit.

The Philistines were a very aggressive, warlike people and are depicted in Egyptian reliefs armed with lances, round shields, long broadswords, and triangular daggers.[5] It is therefore very poignant that Shamgar was armed only with an oxgoad, which is nothing more than a cattle-prod with a sharpened metal tip. A typical oxgoad would be about 1.8m to 2.4m long (6ft to 8ft) with a sharp prickle at one end for driving the oxen, and at the other end a small paddle of iron for scraping the clay from the plough.

The Lord Jesus alluded to the oxgoad when He spoke to Saul of Tarsus on the Damascus Road, "Saul, Saul, why are you persecuting Me? It is hard for you to kick against the goads" (Acts 26:14) or – "It is hard for thee to kick against the pricks" (KJV). Just as a wayward ox would suffer the prick from the prod of the goad at the hands of its driver, so Saul's conscience was being prodded and convicted by the Spirit of God. Happily, as Paul later testified to the Jews at Jerusalem, he was not disobedient to the heavenly vision, but replied, "What shall I do, Lord?" (Acts 22:10). The 'ox goad' had certainly done its job well in the case of Saul of Tarsus. It is also important for us as Christians that we are not violating our conscience in our lives for Him. Let us be sensitive to the leading of the Spirit.

The fact that Shamgar had to use an oxgoad as a weapon is a sad commentary on the impoverished condition of the Israelites. In spite of this dire lack of arms, God gave Shamgar a great victory over the Philistines. An oxgoad against spears, swords and shields! It was exactly as the Hebrew commentator had described the men and women of faith, how they had, "quenched the violence of fire, escaped the edge of the sword, *out of weakness were made strong*, became valiant in battle, turned to flight the armies of the aliens" (Heb 11:34 KJV).

It is a great incentive to remember that God can also use *our* tiny contribution in the work of the gospel and in the service of the saints. Paul has informed us about his own particular case, and how the Lord Jesus had said to him, "My grace is sufficient for you, for My strength is made perfect in weakness." Paul responded with deep resolve, "Therefore most gladly I will rather boast in my infirmities, that the power of Christ may rest upon me" (2 Cor 12:9).

The narrator tells us concerning Shamgar that "he also delivered Israel." We can draw much comfort and encouragement from the mini case study of Shamgar and his ox goad.

---

[5] From entry for "Philistines" in *The New Bible Dictionary* (IVP Reprint 1976).

CHAPTER FOUR

Judges 4:1 – 5:31

Deborah and Barak against the Canaanites

In the days of Deborah, Canaan was like a heavily armed super power in comparison to the weak and unarmed people of Israel. The Israelites were totally outclassed in military technology and expertise. King Jabin's army, commanded by Sisera, had nine hundred iron chariots, and so a conventional battlefield confrontation was out of the question. The Israelites had nothing with which to face such a formidable array of strength and power. We have already noted that a shield or spear could not be found among forty thousand in Israel.

The action for this story takes place in the northern Gentile region of Israel, described at a later time as "The land of Zebulun and the land of Naphtali, toward the sea, across the Jordan, Galilee of the Gentiles" (Matt 4:15). After the death of Ehud the people of Israel again committed evil in the sight of the LORD. On this occasion the LORD sold them into the hand of King Jabin of Canaan, whose throne was in Hazor, a city north of the Sea of Galilee. The Gentiles ruled the Israelites with an iron fist for twenty years. Israel had already known cruel oppression down in Egypt and ought never again to have been oppressed by an ungodly nation Once more in their desperation they "cried out to the LORD" (4:3). The LORD answered their cry in an unexpected way:

> *"In the days of Shamgar, son of Anath,*
> *In the days of Jael,*
> *The highways were deserted,*

And the travellers walked along the byways.
Village life ceased, it ceased in Israel,
Until I, Deborah, arose,
Arose a mother in Israel.
They chose new gods;
Then there was war in the gates;
Not a shield or spear was seen
among forty thousand in Israel.
My heart is with the rulers of Israel
Who offered themselves willingly with the people.
Bless the LORD!

From the *Song of Deborah*, Judges 5:6-9

Deborah is one of the most courageous and inspirational women in the Bible. She was a prophetess, strategist, encourager, poetess, judge and, perhaps most importantly, was in touch with God. The influence of a godly woman is incalculable. We have already observed that the secret of Othniel's strength was his wife. The secret of Israel's deliverance from the Gentile oppressor was not Barak, but Deborah, described as "a mother in Israel" (5:7). This in itself is a commentary on the spiritual state of the nation, as leadership is properly the domain of men. It is irregular for men to be led by a woman, a paradox that Deborah was fully aware of as we shall presently see.

The people of Israel came to Deborah for judgement in the hill country of Ephraim. She would sit under the 'palm of Deborah' located somewhere between Ramah and Bethel. On one such occasion Deborah sent a message for Barak, the son of Abinoam, to report to her for duty. When Barak duly arrived from his home at Kedesh in Naphtali, Deborah recited a message from God for him, "The Lord, the God of Israel, commands you..."

It was not the kind of command that Barak wanted to hear. It was a call to military action. He was told to go and muster ten thousand men from the tribes of Naphtali and Zebulun and to gather them on Mount Tabor. The LORD would then draw General Sisera and his army, complete with chariots, to the River Kishon for battle. God promised Barak, "I will deliver him into your hand" (4:7).

Humanly speaking, it would be a very unequal match. Sisera was the seasoned campaigner of a well-equipped standing army, while Barak was an amateur soldier leading a poorly armed volunteer militia. Poor Barak was in a dilemma. His response was to insist that Deborah accompany him in person to the battle field, otherwise he would not go. Deborah agreed to Barak's plea, but pointed out that the honour for the victory over Sisera would not go to Barak, but to a woman. Notwithstanding, Barak went and summoned the men of Zebulun and Naphtali to report to Kedesh. The people answered the call. Barak and the army of ten thousand, accompanied by Deborah, made their way to the barren slopes of Mount Tabor.

The Battle of the River Kishon

It appears to have been Heber the Kenite who informed Sisera that Barak, with an Israelite army, had mobilised on Mount Tabor. It is difficult to know whether or not Deborah had confided in Heber and brought him into the game-plan. Either way, Sisera reacted exactly as Deborah had wanted. Sisera called his entire army with all the chariots, from Harosheth of the Gentiles, to the River Kishon. As the Israelites looked down from the mountainside of Tabor toward the Jezreel Valley, they could see the massed army of Sisera assembled at the River Kishon. The time for action had come.

At the right moment Deborah, a master of strategy and tactics, told Barak to begin operations, "Up! For this is the day in which the LORD has delivered Sisera into your hand. Has not the LORD gone out before you?" (4:14). Perhaps Deborah had already seen the rain clouds on the horizon! While the Israelites were on Mount Tabor, they were safe from Sisera's chariots. Sisera wanted to meet the Israelites down on the plain where he knew he could annihilate them. At Deborah's word, and to Sisera's delight, Barak led the army of ten thousand volunteer soldiers down the mountainside and toward the enemy. As the Canaanites prepared to counter-attack and meet their assailants head-on, they had an unexpected difficulty in manoeuvring the chariots. A sudden downpour of rain had turned the dry Kishon river bed into a rushing torrent. In their book *Battles of the Bible*, the Jewish writers Herzog and Gichon had this to say,

"A sudden downpour aided the Israelites considerably and helped turn Sisera's defeat into a rout. The Song of Deborah speaks explicitly of heavenly intervention and tells how the Kishon River rose and swept away in its torrent the enemy's horses and chariots. It should be explained that sudden rainfall, often at a substantial distance, can fill the dry river beds or turn docile streams into a pouring torrent that appears suddenly and sweeps down with deadly force on anything and anybody caught unawares. To this we must add the sudden local downpour that did much to hinder those of the much-dreaded 'chariots of iron' not caught by the torrent itself. Even the heavily armed infantry must have become bogged down and hampered in their movements."[6]

The iron chariots in which the Canaanites had put their faith, proved to be their undoing as they quickly lost their mobility in wet, swampy conditions. The Israelites quickly overwhelmed the Canaanites who by now were attempting to retreat. It would seem that the Israelites had little difficulty in pursuing the chariots in the rainfall. The narrator informs us, "But Barak pursued after the chariots, and after the host, unto Harosheth of the Gentiles: and all the host of Sisera fell upon the edge of the sword; and there was not a man left." (4:16 KJV).

Proud Sisera did not earn any medals for gallantry on that day. The Commander-in-Chief of King Jabin's army alighted from his chariot, deserted his men, and ran away. He continued running until, exhausted and thirsty, he reached the tent of Jael, the wife of Heber. That was most unfortunate for Sisera. Not only had he failed spectacularly that day in his military leadership, but now he was about to fall into a woman's trap. Jael invited him into her tent assuring him that there was nothing to fear. She lavished hospitality on him, covering him with a rug and refreshing him with milk. Sisera instructed his hostess, "Stand at the door of the tent, and if any man comes and asks you, 'Is there any man here?' you shall say, No" (4:20). Believing all was well, Sisera fell fast asleep.

Perhaps, in peacetime, Jael would have made a very good neighbour. She had probably shown old-fashioned 'Bedouin' hospitality to many a desert wanderer in the past - but this was not peacetime. As Solomon observed, for everything there is a season. There is, "a time to love, and a time to hate; a time of war, and a time of peace" (Eccl 3:8). Jael would have known that the death of Sisera would bring final closure on the war with Jabin, and ensure Israel's deliverance from its oppressor. The sympathies of Heber and Jael are not actually articulated anywhere in the narrative, but their actions certainly seem to indicate their support for the Israelite uprising. Jael quite literally struck a blow for Israel by driving a tent peg through Sisera's brain!

Barak was, in all likelihood, feeling much better as the day went on. Perhaps he was wondering why he had ever doubted God, but was now sensing a historic victory. He had only one more thing to do that day to crown his achievement, and that was to catch up with Sisera and take him, dead or alive. As he was pursuing his prey, Jael came out to meet him, "Come, I will show you the man whom you seek" (4:22). Barak followed Jael into the tent and saw the dead body of Sisera with the tent peg through his temple. Perhaps, at that moment, Barak recalled the words of Deborah. The glory and honour for proud Sisera's destruction would not go to Barak, but to a tent-dwelling woman named Jael.

The vital step now for the Israelites was to consolidate their victory. It has been said in more recent times, "Modern military doctrine therefore stresses planning for the exploitation of a victory, which has become an integral phase in any operation, including the allocation of troops and means for this purpose as early as the planning stage."[7] One suspects that if such a plan existed for the Israelites, it would owe more to Deborah than to Barak. God had subdued Jabin the king of Canaan that day before all the people of Israel. Sisera was dead and his army destroyed. But there was yet more to be done to fully exploit the victory. To have stopped at that point could have been disastrous. The narrator tells us, "And the hand of the children of Israel grew stronger and stronger against Jabin the king of Canaan, until they had destroyed Jabin king of Canaan" (4:24). The Canaanite oppression was over and the land had rest for forty years.

The Song of Deborah

There must have been great rejoicing throughout the northern half of Israel as they realised the extent of their victory. God had enabled them to defeat an army of 900 chariots, and both King Jabin and General Sisera were dead.   The Gentile yoke had at last been broken and the people of Israel could once again travel safely on the highways of Israel. Whether there were street parties or bonfires we do not know, but there was certainly singing. We have the full record of the magnificent song of victory sung by Deborah and Barak on that day. The song divides neatly into three parts.

Part One: To Deborah and Barak (5:1-12)

The honour is given to the LORD from the very beginning of the song:

> *When the leaders lead in Israel,*
> *When the people willingly offer themselves,*
> *Bless the LORD!*

(Verses 2-3)

Deborah is deeply thankful to the LORD for the response of the nation, and gives all the glory to God. The poem recalls the similar events that took place at Mount Seir and Mount Sinai when Israel was heading for the Promised Land. In verses 6-9, the dire circumstances of Israel are recalled, circumstances that pertained until Deborah arose as "a mother in Israel." The willingness of the leaders of Israel to rise to the occasion is again the subject of rejoicing and thanksgiving. Deborah leaves us in no doubt as to the reason for the recurrence of war in the gates – it was the people's choice of new gods, "They chose new gods; then there was war in the gates" (5:8).

In verses 10-11, the song calls on both the rich people and the peasantry to tell of the Lord's deliverance. Those who ride on tawny asses, and those who sit on rich carpets are exhorted to sing. Those who now walk safely on the highways ought to be singing. The musicians at the watering places repeat the triumphs of the LORD and of the peasantry in Israel.

The song suddenly takes us back to the day of the battle, recalling the march of the people of the LORD to the gates, and the rallying call to Deborah and Barak:

Awake, awake, Deborah:
Awake, awake, utter a song:Arise, Barak, and lead thy captivity
captive, Thou son of Abinoam.

(Verse 12 KJV)

From the side of Mount Tabor, Barak was able to see the oppressors of his people gathered at the River Kishon. The people of Israel had been held captive by a ruthless Gentile regime for 20 years. Captivity had been a hard experience for Israel, but here was now an opportunity for Barak to effect a complete reversal. He was about to make captives of those who had held his people in captivity. It was a sweet moment for Barak to rise and lead away his captors as captives.

The Psalmist uses similar language as he describes that future moment of triumph when the LORD will come in millennial power (Ps 68:18). In the New Testament, Paul alludes to the language of Judges 5 and Psalm 68, when describing the triumphant ascent of the risen Lord Jesus far above all heavens.

43

He had put away sin; He had conquered death; He had destroyed the works of the devil. The very things that had held men in cruel captivity were now led captive. In celebration of His triumph and His grace, He gave gifts to men for their blessing: some apostles, some prophets, some evangelists, some pastors and some teachers. These gifts to the church are to equip the saints for the work of ministry, and for the building up of the body of Christ.

Part Two: To the People of the LORD (5:13-23)

The various responses of the different tribes are now recorded for posterity. Ephraim followed Benjamin nobly into the valley to face the enemy. Zebulun and Issachar rushed into the valley at the heels of Barak. On the other hand, Reuben hesitated and stayed among the sheepfolds. The tribe of Manasseh remained on the other side of the Jordan, while Dan stayed with his ships, and Asher sat still at the sea. But special commendation is given to Zebulun and Naphtali, who risked their lives in the thick of the battle.

How shall we be assessed at the Judgement Seat of Christ, when every saint will receive his or her commendation from the Lord? Shall we be included among those who, like Reuben, searched their hearts so much that they ended up doing nothing? Or shall we be like Zebulun and Naphtali who jeopardised their lives to the death?

Not only were kings fighting at Taanach by the waters of Megiddo, but the very stars and rivers were fighting against Sisera. The onrushing torrent of the Kishon River was also part of heaven's plan to deliver the Lord's people. Both heaven and nature were on the side of Israel! A curse was reserved for Meroz, whose inhabitants refused to come to the help of the Lord.

Part Three: To Jael (5:24-31)

The slaying of Sisera by Jael is a special cause for rejoicing. Sisera represented everything that was cruel, oppressive and Gentile. Jael had the courage to outwit and destroy the enemy of Israel. She was a tent-dwelling woman with a mallet and a tent peg which she used to deadly effect. The great Gentile brain was crushed, shattered and pierced. Mighty Sisera, who had commanded an army of nine hundred chariots, now lay dead at the feet of Jael.

The graphic portrayal of Sisera's mother waiting for his return is poignant and tragic. She remains in denial about the reality of Sisera's defeat and makes herself believe that he is taking his time in dividing the spoil. Her reference to "a maiden or two for every man" is indicative of the kind of tyrannical and licentious rule associated with Jabin and Sisera. That was exactly the kind of tyranny in which Jael had played such an important part in crushing. At the end of the day, the LORD's enemies will surely perish, while the LORD's friends will be like the sun as he rises in his might. God blessed the faith of Deborah, Barak, and Jael by granting the land rest for 40 years.

Dissecting the Gentile Mind

Jabin and Sisera represented everything that was Gentile and estranged from God. Gentile technology far surpassed that of Israel – the Canaanites had nine hundred chariots. It is emphasised that Sisera came from Harosheth "of the Gentiles". The dominant culture and mindset was Gentile. The name Jabin means 'intelligent'. *The Canaanite Gentiles are a symbol of the intelligence and wisdom of this world.* The New Testament contains important warnings against imbibing Gentile values.

Gentile religion – how not to pray

The Lord Jesus had this to say about Gentile forms of prayer: "And when you pray, do not heap up empty phrases as the Gentiles do, for they think that they will be heard for their many words. Do not be like them, for your Father knows what you need before you ask Him" (Matt 6:7-8 ESV). The Lord went on to teach His disciples how to pray regarding such things as holiness, the coming kingdom, the Father's will, daily food, forgiveness, preservation, and deliverance (Matt 6:9-13). Prayer was to be a meaningful communion between the believer and his God. It was not to be a meaningless repetition of phrases. It is a sad irony that many in mainstream Christendom have taken this model prayer and have used it verbatim as a meaningless repetition. Let us make sure that our prayer-life does not deteriorate to that of the heathen.

Gentile values – "do not be like them"

The Lord Jesus was urging His disciples not to be anxious in relation to the material necessities of life such as food, drink and clothing. Such things ought not to be the chief aim and occupation in life. In today's 'Gentile' world, there is a multi-billion pound industry based on people's preoccupation with food and fashion. That is what many people in the world live for. Food, drink, and clothing still take first place in the minds and lives of modern Gentiles.

The Christian should live for a radically different value system. The first priority in life for the believer is to seek the kingdom of God and His righteousness, "Therefore I say to you, do not worry about your life, what you will eat or what you will drink; nor about your body, what you will put on. Is not life more than food and the body more than clothing? Look at the birds of the air, for they neither sow nor reap nor gather into barns; yet your heavenly Father feeds them. Are you not of more value than they? Which of you by worrying can add one cubit to his stature? So why do you worry about clothing? Consider the lilies of the field, how they grow: they neither toil nor spin; and yet I say to you that even Solomon in all his glory was not arrayed like one of these. Now if God so clothes the grass of the field, which today is, and tomorrow is thrown into the oven, will He not much more clothe you, O you of little faith? Therefore do not worry, saying, 'What shall we eat?' or 'What shall we drink?' or 'What shall we wear?' For after all these things the Gentiles seek. For your heavenly Father knows that you need all these things. But seek first the kingdom of God and His righteousness, and all these things shall be added to you" (Matt 6:25-33).

When your unconverted neighbours and colleagues observe your conduct and lifestyle, do they see someone who lives for a totally different set of aims and values?

Gentile ambition – "It shall not be so among you"

The Lord Jesus warned of yet another feature of Gentile lifestyle and values. Gentiles love to have power and control over others. Some of the disciples also had wanted such recognition of status and importance. The mother of James and John was so ambitious for her two sons that she wanted the Lord to honour them above the other disciples in the future kingdom. When the other ten reacted with indignation, the Lord Jesus called the disciples to Him and said, "You know that the rulers of the Gentiles lord it over them, and those who are great exercise authority over them. Yet it shall not be so among you; but whoever desires to become great among you, let him be your servant. And whoever desires to be first among you, let him be your slave – just as the Son of man did not come to be served, but to serve, and to give His life a ransom for many" (Matt 20:25-28).

How important it is that love of power and control is kept out of the local church. There is no place for an ecclesiastical hierarchy of power in a Biblically gathered church. We are to serve one another and to love one another. In this we are to follow Christ's example, not that of the Gentiles.

Gentile thinking - "You did not so learn Christ"

Paul tells the Ephesian believers that the thinking of the Gentile mind is futile, darkened, alienated from God, ignorant, hardened and callous. Our thought-life will eventually impact on our behaviour. The Gentiles have given themselves up to immorality and uncleanness. Paul writes, "This I say, therefore, and testify in the Lord, that you should no longer walk as the rest of the Gentiles walk, in the futility of their mind, having their understanding darkened, being alienated from the life of God, because of the ignorance that is in them, because of the blindness of their heart; who, being past feeling, have given

47

themselves over to lewdness, to work all uncleanness with greediness. But you have not so learned Christ, if indeed you have heard Him and have been taught by Him, as the truth is in Jesus" (Eph 4:17-21)

Gentile conduct – "let the time that is past suffice"

Peter warned his readers to have nothing to do with the indulgent and sinful conduct associated with Gentiles, "For we have spent enough of our past lifetime in doing the will of the Gentiles - when we walked in lewdness, lusts, drunkenness, revelries, drinking parties, and abominable idolatries. In regard to these, they think it strange that you do not run with them in the same flood of dissipation, speaking evil of you. They will give an account to Him who is ready to judge the living and the dead" (1 Pet 4:3-5).

What is the main lesson that we can learn from the story of Deborah, Barak and Jael? Surely it is to guard against reverting to a Gentile way of thinking. If ever we find ourselves praying like a Gentile, or living for earthly values, or promoting self, or behaving in an unbecoming way, let us act quickly and decisively like Jael, and drive a tent peg through our Gentile mindset! Let us be transformed by the renewal of our minds. Paul, when writing to the Corinthians, makes a striking contrast between the wisdom of this world and the wisdom of God. In the context of the preaching of the cross, Paul writes:
"Where is the wise? Where is the scribe? Where is the disputer of this age? Has not God made foolish the wisdom of this world? For since, in the wisdom of God, the world through wisdom did not know God, it pleased God through the foolishness of the message preached to save those who believe. For Jews request a sign, and Greeks seek after wisdom; but we preach Christ crucified, to the Jews a stumbling block and to the Greeks foolishness, but to those who are called, both Jews and Greeks, Christ the power of God and the wisdom of God" (1 Cor 1:20-24).

We finish this chapter with the intriguing observation that

the Lord Jesus lived in the region of Zebulun and Naphtali. A greater than Barak had come to live among them. Matthew quotes Isaiah the prophet (Mt 4:12-16),

"Now when Jesus heard that John had been put in prison, He departed to Galilee. And leaving Nazareth, He came and dwelt in Capernaum, which is by the sea, in the regions of Zebulun and Naphtali, that it might be fulfilled which was spoken by Isaiah the prophet, saying:

"The land of Zebulun and the land of Naphtali,
By the way of the sea, beyond the Jordan, Galilee of the Gentiles:
The people who sat in darkness have seen a great light,
And upon those who sat in the region and shadow of death
Light has dawned."

---

[6] Herzog, Chaim and Gichon, Mordechai *Battles of the Bible* (Greenhill Books, London, 1997, p.69).
[7] Ibid p.56.

CHAPTER FIVE

Judges 6:1 – 8:35

Gideon against the Midianites

We are all familiar with the playground bully who makes the lives of vulnerable children a misery. The bully is driven by a desire for power over others, and takes pleasure in inflicting physical and mental suffering in an unequal contest of strength. The same phenomenon often happens between nations. History is full of examples of empires and tyrants who have imposed despotic and cruel rule on smaller and weaker nations. In extreme cases, the conquering power has exploited and tyrannised the subject people with malice and hatred. The desire to inflict suffering on defenceless victims is one of the lowest forms of debased human behaviour.

Midian was a son of Abraham by his concubine Keturah and became a desert dweller in the southern region of Transjordan. The Midianites, who were often associated culturally with the Ishmaelites, had once joined with Moabites in hiring Balaam to curse the people of Israel. Not only were Midianites inveterate enemies of the LORD's people, they were also cruel and pitiless bullies.

Midian means 'strife'. Humiliated by the Midianites, the people of Israel were reduced to living in mountain hideouts, caves and strongholds. When the Israelites planted crops, the Midianites in their malevolence, along with Amalekites and other eastern people, would attack Israel and destroy the produce of the land. The narrator records that the Midianites, along with their cattle, tents and camels, would waste the land as they trampled and flattened it in huge numbers. Israel was powerless to resist this neighbouring bully.

Why did the people of Israel find themselves in such deprived and impoverished conditions? After all, they were in a land which should have been flowing with milk and honey. Once again, the people had reverted to evil, and so the LORD had given them into the hands of Midian for seven years. The people of Israel, in their misery and humiliation, cried to the LORD for deliverance. The LORD responded initially by sending an unnamed prophet who spoke on God's behalf, accusing the people of unfaithfulness,

"This is what the LORD, the God of Israel, says: I brought you up out of Egypt, out of the land of slavery. I snatched you from the power of Egypt and from the hand of all your oppressors. I drove them from before you and gave you their land. I said to you, 'I am the LORD your God; do not worship the gods of the Amorites, in whose land you live.' But you have not listened to me." (6:8-10).

Nevertheless, God responded by raising one of Israel's greatest heroes - Gideon, the son of Joash the Abiezrite.

The Call of Gideon

We are introduced to Gideon while he is beating out wheat in a wine press. That was an unusual place to be threshing wheat, but then these were unusual times. Gideon was hiding the wheat from the Midianites and was risking his life to ensure that the LORD's people had food. What a striking indicator of the character of the man! Many Christian leaders in more recent times, living under anti-Christian regimes, have had to risk their lives by teaching and preaching the word of God in secret to fellow national believers.

While Gideon was working with the wheat, the angel of the LORD came and sat under an oak tree at Ophrah, which belonged to Gideon's father, Joash the Abiezrite. The angel appeared to Gideon with this stirring greeting, "The LORD is with you, you mighty man of valour" (6:12). Gideon responded by enquiring why such misfortune had befallen Israel if the LORD was with them. If indeed the LORD had brought Israel out of Egypt, why had He now forsaken them? The LORD did not answer Gideon's questions at that moment. Perhaps he was not ready for the answers. Instead the LORD gave Gideon an unmistakable call to service, "Go in this might of yours, and you shall save Israel from the hand of the Midianites. Have I not sent you?" (6:14). Gideon protested that his clan was the weakest in Manasseh, and that he was least in his father's house. This was not mock humility, but a genuine sense of inadequacy and weakness on Gideon's part. Gideon is the kind of man that God uses - humble and self-effacing rather than proud and self-confident. The LORD gave Gideon his answer, "But I will be with you, and you shall defeat the Midianites as one man."

How was Gideon to know if it really was the LORD who was speaking to him? Perhaps we all like the kind of assurance and re-assurance that Gideon craved. He wanted a sign so that he could be absolutely certain. Which of us could fault him for that? There is surely a vast difference between rank unbelief on the one hand, and faith reaching out for assurance on the other. At any rate, the LORD was very patient with Gideon and granted him time to prepare food and seek a sign of confirmation.

Gideon quickly began cooking a meal from food which he had been hiding carefully from the Midianites. This was not fast convenience food, but a royal banquet lovingly prepared. At last Gideon brought out his gift to the LORD - a young goat, unleavened bread, and broth. The goat meat was presented in a basket and the broth served in a pot. The LORD instructed Gideon to put the meat and bread on a rock and to pour the broth over them. When Gideon had done so, the angel of the LORD reached out the tip of his staff and touched the meat and the unleavened cakes. What happened next must have come as a great shock to Gideon. The narrator tells us that flames sprang from the rock and consumed the meat and the unleavened cakes, at which moment the angel of the LORD vanished out of his sight.

Gideon was overwhelmed as he realised the immensity of what he had just witnessed. He had seen the angel of the LORD face to face. Such a thing is not the normal experience of mortal men, and Gideon exclaimed with fear, "Alas, O LORD God! For I have seen the Angel of the LORD face to face" (6:22). Gideon, having concluded that he was doomed, must have been greatly relieved to hear words of grace and acceptance coming from the LORD Himself, "Peace be with you; do not fear: you shall not die." Gideon's response was to worship by building an altar to the LORD and calling it "The LORD is Peace".

Starting in one's own house

The practice of idolatry in Israel was not rare and occasional, but rather widespread and endemic. Virtually every home seems to have been affected, and Gideon's house was no exception. Gideon's first task was in some ways his hardest one – he had to destroy the altar that his own father had built. If Gideon was going to do something great for God on the national level, he would first have to show faithfulness to God in his own home and among his own townspeople. The LORD commanded Gideon, "Take your father's young bull, the second bull of seven years old, and tear down the altar of Baal that your father has, and cut down the wooden image that is beside it; and build an altar to the LORD your God on top of this rock in the proper arrangement, and take the second bull and offer a burnt sacrifice with the wood of the image which you shall cut down" (6:25-26).

This was no easy task and Gideon was too frightened to carry out the command in daylight. We are told that because he was afraid of his family and the men of the town, he did not make his move until night had fallen. He took ten men of his servants and did as the LORD had told him. This would seem to indicate that Gideon's family was relatively well off in that they had at least ten servants. Gideon's father Joash had taken the initiative to build an altar to Baal and to grow a grove of trees. The townspeople had evidently been worshipping Baal at the altar of Joash. Not only had Joash led his own household astray, but he had led his neighbours astray. How profoundly sad to use one's influence and privilege to lead other people away from the true and living God!

When darkness had descended on the town of Ophrah, the covert mission began in earnest. Gideon and the ten servants set at work demolishing the pagan altar stone by stone, and cutting down the image of Ashtoreth. Soon there was nothing left to remind anyone that Baal had once been worshipped there. While this was going on, a new altar was being built on top of the rock with the stones being carefully placed in order. The cut wood from the Astoreth was then placed on the new altar. The night's proceedings were finally completed when Gideon, in accordance with the LORD's command, offered his father's second bull as a burnt offering. As the flames of the altar lit up the night sky, there was at least one man in Israel who had forsaken Baal and had returned to the God of his fathers.

While the sun was shedding its morning rays across the land, the early risers of Ophrah were shocked to find that the altar to Baal had been demolished and the trees of the Ashtoreth cut down. The people immediately began their investigations to find the culprit, and it wasn't long until all the evidence was pointing to Gideon. A delegation of townspeople made their way to the house of Joash and demanded that he bring out his son so that they could put him to death.

When a believer makes a bold stand for God, others will often be encouraged to do the same. Joash would have to make a choice, whether to continue serving Baal or to follow his son's courageous example. As the neighbours were pressing him to hand over his son, Joash distanced himself from Baal and, like Gideon, took sides with the God of his fathers. Joash had evidently been totally disillusioned regarding the worship of Baal. His son had shown everyone that Baal was nothing more than myth, a make-believe god that was powerless to save himself or anyone else. The reaction of Gideon's father was both courageous and right.

"Would you plead for Baal?" Joash asked all the men who confronted him, "Would you save him?" His boldness was increasing by the moment as he warned that any who would contend for Baal would be put to death by morning. His final thrust was a mocking and defiant challenge directed at Baal himself, "If he is a god, let him plead for himself, because his altar has been torn down."

Joash had been deceived by Canaanite religion, but now his eyes were opened. His recovery was in great measure due to his son's stand for the living God. Gideon's testimony was not only an example and blessing to his own father, but was also a tremendous voice to his townspeople. In fact, he made such an impression on the men of Ophrah that they gave him a new name, Jerubbaal, which means "Let Baal plead against him, because he has torn down his altar."

In our own day, the idea of religious pluralism would urge us that all belief systems are equally valid and that no one system has a monopoly on truth. Our generation needs men like Gideon, who will preach a true and scriptural gospel, and be fearless examples for others to follow.

Gideon's action in his own home had prepared him for a far greater danger at the national level. The Midianites, Amalekites and people of the East crossed the Jordan and encamped in the Valley of Jezreel. Once again they intended to humiliate and impoverish the people of Israel, but this time God was going to act on behalf of His people. We read the striking words, "But the Spirit of the LORD came upon Gideon" (6:34). Normally, when the Midianites arrived, the Israelites would brace themselves for the worst and retreat to their mountain dens and caves, while at the same time trying to hide what food and livestock they had. On this occasion a different note was sounding through the land. Gideon's trumpet was calling the

Abiezrites to gather for battle. Messengers were sent throughout Gideon's tribe of Manasseh, and also to the tribes of Asher, Zebulun and Naphtali. It wasn't long until an army of about thirty two thousand men had rallied to Jerubbaal, the man who had broken down the altar of Baal.

Gideon and the fleece

When Gideon saw the army and considered the momentous task that lay before him, he seemed to have had second thoughts about the whole enterprise. In other words, he was losing his nerve and needed reassurance. Gideon asked God to confirm if He really was going to deliver Israel by his hand. Gideon proposed to put a woollen fleece on the threshing floor overnight. If the dew settled on the fleece, but not on the ground, Gideon would know that God would save Israel by his hand. The next morning the fleece was soaked with dew, while the floor was perfectly dry. But that was still not enough for Gideon and he now proposed apologetically for the test to be replicated but with reverse results. This time he wanted the fleece to remain dry while there was dew on the ground round about. That night God did as Gideon had requested, and Gideon's heart must have been deeply moved the following morning as he discovered the fleece to be dry and the ground to be wet with dew. There could be no doubt that God was going to keep His word to Gideon.

This raises the question as to how believers today can know and be assured that they are in the centre of God's will. Is it necessary today to devise tests and signs as Gideon did? How can we know God's will? The first step is to prayerfully read the word of God and we will find that numerous aspects of God's will for us are already plainly written, for example:

The will of God – *your consecration*

"I beseech you therefore, brethren, by the mercies of God, that you present your bodies a living sacrifice, holy, acceptable to God, which is your reasonable service. And do not be conformed to this world: but be transformed by the renewing of your mind, that you may prove what is that good and acceptable and perfect will of God" (Rom 12:1-2).

The will of God – *your sanctification*

"For this is the will of God, your sanctification, that you should abstain from sexual immorality..." (1 Thess 4:3).

The will of God – *your commitment to your employer*

"Bondservants, be obedient to those who are your masters according to the flesh, with fear and trembling, in singleness of your heart, as to Christ; not with eyeservice, as men-pleasers; but as the bondservants of Christ, doing the will of God from the heart..." (Eph 6:5-6).

The will of God – *your good conduct as a citizen*

"Therefore submit yourselves to every ordinance of man for the Lord's sake: whether to the king as supreme; or to governors, as to those who are sent by him for the punishment of evildoers, and for the praise of them that do good. For this is the will of God, that by doing good you may put to silence the ignorance of foolish men..." (1 Pet 2:13-15).

There are other issues which do not require any further guidance than we already have, e.g. baptism. As for the believer who feels called to special service, guidance will come from the scriptures, prayerful exercise, encouragements from fellow believers, and an open door of opportunity. For the Christian, there is no greater joy and contentment than knowing that we are in the centre of God's will for us. The Lord Jesus said, "My food is to do the will of Him who sent me, and to finish His work" (John 4:34).

Down-sizing the army

Napoleon is attributed with the famous observation that God is on the side of the big battalions. Although Napoleon was undoubtedly being cynical, nevertheless it is generally true to say that the chances of victory in a battle are often weighed in favour of the larger army. Any military leader or battle-field commander will take great comfort in the superior size of his fighting force. It is not recorded what went through Gideon's mind when the LORD told him that He would not be able to give the Midianites into his hand because his army was too big! The problem was that the people would give themselves the credit for the victory.

On the LORD's instructions, Gideon announced to the army that if any were too frightened to fight, they were free to return to their homes. This immediately reduced the army from thirty-two thousand to ten thousand. Gideon was possibly beginning to feel seriously disadvantaged at this point, but there was more to come. God told Gideon to take the remaining ten thousand men to the water edge to drink and that He would test them there. Those who knelt down and lapped the water from the surface with their tongues were dismissed. Those who lapped the water from their hands were chosen to fight. This procedure had now reduced the army to a mere three hundred men. Humanly speaking, this could not have made much sense to Gideon. However, the LORD assured Gideon, "With the three hundred men who lapped I will save you and give the Midianites into your hand, and let all the others go every man to his home" (7:7).

There is great comfort in knowing that God will never ask us to do anything that is beyond our capability. He knows and understands our limitations. The size of the Midianite army was one hundred and thirty-five thousand against Gideon's task force of three hundred. God knew that Gideon was afraid and in need of strengthening. On the night that the battle was to take place, God told Gideon to first take his servant Purah and make a pre-battle visit to the edge of the Midianite camp. He was to listen to what the Midianites were saying and he would be strengthened.

We do not read of Purah doing anything else other than accompanying Gideon on his reconnaissance mission. That may seem like a fairly insignificant role, yet Gideon in all probability would not have gone alone. Sometimes we can strengthen the hand of a believer simply by standing with them in their work for God, just as Purah did.

The narrator's description of the enemy camp is striking. We are told that the Midianites, and the Amalekites, and the people of the East lay along the valley like swarming locusts. In addition, their camels were in number like the sand on the seashore. As Gideon and Purah reached the outpost of the camp, they overheard a conversation in which one man was telling a comrade about his puzzling dream in which a barley cake had rolled into the Midianite camp and had flattened a tent. The comrade replied that this was no other than the sword of Gideon, the son of Joash, a man of Israel. Gideon listened as the man concluded that God was about to give the whole camp into his hand. The heart of Gideon bowed with worship on hearing such confirmation. He no longer had a shadow of a doubt that God was going to deliver Midian into his hand.

The Battle of Light and Darkness

Gideon returned to the camp of Israel and immediately began to organise and brief his army. He divided the three hundred men into three equal companies and equipped them for the battle. The men must have been puzzled when they received their battle kit. Instead of receiving combat weapons as one might have expected, each man was given a trumpet, a torch and an empty earthen jar. "When I come to the edge of the camp, do as I do" instructed Gideon, "When I blow the trumpet, I and all who are with me, then you also blow the trumpets on every side of the whole camp and say, 'The sword of the LORD and of Gideon'" (7:17-18).

The three companies silently made their way in darkness to their planned positions at the edge of the enemy camp. Gideon's band came to the outskirt of the camp just as they changed guards for the middle watch. The element of surprise would be critical in unnerving the unsuspecting Midianites. Gideon chose his timing so that the new watch would not have had time to adjust their eyes and ears to the night.[8] Gideon and his men took the lead by breaking the jars, holding up the torches in their left hand and shouting "The sword of the LORD and of Gideon." Then, lifting the trumpets with their right hands, they sounded a prolonged battle call. This gave the signal to the other groups who also smashed the jars, blew the trumpets and held up the torches. Panic and fear broke out in the camp while the three hundred Israelites stood their ground blowing the trumpets and holding up their torches. The noise of smashing pitchers, the light from the torches, and the blasts of the trumpets caused total confusion among the Midianites who, while they were screaming and fleeing, also began slaying one another. The sight and sound of stampeding camels would have added to the pandemonium. We are told that the "LORD set every man's sword against his companion throughout the whole camp" (7:22). The Midianite army, now defeated, demoralised and frightened, fled in full retreat toward the River Jordan.

The picture of men breaking earthen vessels, blowing trumpets and hiding behind the light, becomes a very powerful symbol taken up by Paul in reference to the gospel. The apostle is evidently alluding, at least in part, to the story of Gideon when he writes the following:

"But even if our gospel is veiled, it is veiled to those who are perishing, whose minds the god of this age has blinded, who do not believe, lest the light of the gospel of the glory of Christ, who is the image of God, should shine on them. For we do not preach ourselves, but Christ Jesus the Lord, and ourselves your bondservants for Jesus' sake. For it is the God who commanded light to shine out of darkness, who has shone in our hearts to give the light of the knowledge of the glory of God in the face of Jesus Christ. But we have this treasure in earthen vessels, that the excellence of the power may be of God and not of us." (2 Cor 4:3-7).

The unbeliever is described as lost, his mind being in a condition of blindness and darkness. This blindness is caused by the god of this world who wants to keep the unbeliever from seeing the light of the gospel of the glory of Christ, who is the image of God. But just as in creation God commanded light to shine out of darkness, so God has shone in the hearts of those who believe with the light of the knowledge of the glory of God in the face of Jesus Christ.

There are some helpful analogies between one of Gideon's soldiers and a gospel preacher. Firstly, the soldier had the torch in the earthen vessel; Paul says we too have the treasure in earthen vessels. Secondly, the soldier had to smash the earthen vessel and hide behind the light; Paul says we preach not ourselves but Jesus Christ as Lord. The preacher must be careful not to promote himself, but to hide behind the message. Thirdly, the soldier had to hold up the torch so that the light would penetrate the darkness of the night; the preacher too has a light to hold up – the light of the glorious gospel of Christ which shines into the human heart, dispelling the darkness and giving the light of the knowledge of the glory of God in the face of Jesus Christ. Fourthly, the soldier had a trumpet to blow which could be heard far and wide; the preacher is to herald and proclaim the message to the whole creation.

The gospel of Christ is God's last word to this age. After two thousand years, the gospel is still being proclaimed throughout the world, saving lives and changing destinies. The Midianite army had to retreat from the Israelites on seeing the lights and hearing the trumpets. Let us remind ourselves that the gospel is still the power of God to salvation for everyone who believes. Gideon's army was reduced from thirty-two thousand to three hundred so that the people were unable to say that they had won a victory by their own power. How important it is to keep preaching Christ, and to remember that the excellency of the power is of God and not of us!

The Mopping Up Operation

The Midianites were in total disarray as they fled in the night in the direction of the River Jordan. This was part of Gideon's strategic battle plan which he accomplished by surrounding the Midianites on three sides of a rectangle while leaving one side open to allow the enemy to retreat toward the south east. Everything was going perfectly to plan. The people of Naphtali, Asher and Manasseh were called to pursue the fleeing army. Gideon also sent messengers throughout the hill country of Ephraim, asking them to come down against the Midianites and take the waters against them.

The Ephraimites instantly rallied to the call and had swift and spectacular success. They began by capturing the waters as far as Beth Barah and also the Jordan. However, their most impressive achievement that day was to capture and execute two of the princes of Midian - Oreb and Zeeb. One execution took place at a rock which would subsequently be known as the rock of Oreb, while the other was carried out at a winepress which would become known as the winepress of Zeeb. After pursuing the Midianites further, the men of Ephraim eventually returned across the Jordan and proudly presented the heads of Oreb and Zeeb to Gideon.

Astonishingly, the Ephraimites were not happy. Inter-tribal tensions began to surface as the men of Ephraim complained fiercely to Gideon that they had not been called at the beginning of the battle. Gideon had originally recruited from Manasseh, Asher, Zebulun and Naphtali. Instead of rejoicing in what had been accomplished, the Ephraimites were suffering from that most primal of human sins – envy. Gideon was only able to placate them by appealing to their vanity and persuading them that they had achieved far more than what he had done. After all, God had given two princes into the hands of the Ephraimites. "What have I been able to do in comparison with you?" protested Gideon. The anger of the Ephraimites subsided when he said this.

Envy was Cain's motive for murdering Abel, and also Saul's motive for harming David. Jealousy and envy can still cause horrendous problems among the Lord's people. How do we feel if another preacher sees much more blessing and fruit than we do? Do we experience feelings of resentment? How do we react when a younger Christian overtakes us in gift and blessing? Jealousy and envy are closely linked to that other deadly sin – pride. In the local church context, envy, jealousy and pride lead to strife, division and factionalism. These were the problems in the church at Corinth. May God grant us grace to rejoice in the blessing and fruit of others.

Gideon and his three hundred men crossed over the River Jordan pursuing hard after the Midianites. They were exhausted by the time they reached Succoth, a city of the tribe of Gad. Gideon requested food for his men, "Please give loaves of bread to the people who follow me, for they are exhausted, and I am pursuing after Zebah and Zalmunna, the kings of Midian" (8:5). The officials of Succoth treated Gideon with contempt, chiding him with the fact that Zebah and Zalmunna were not yet defeated. The bread was refused.

The men of Succoth were sitting on the fence and would not take sides until they knew who would ultimately win the struggle. This was a cowardly response. May God help us to take the LORD's side regardless of the consequences.

Gideon was outraged at this rebuff and promised the officials of Succoth that on his return from the victory over Zebah and Zalmunna, he would flail their flesh with thorns and briers. He continued to the nearby city of Penuel where, on making the same request, was again refused. This time Gideon promised to return and break down the tower of the city.

The Midianites had lost one hundred and twenty thousand men in the battle, reducing the size of the army from one hundred and thirty-five thousand to a mere fifteen thousand men. Gideon and his men continued their pursuit until they finally caught up with the depleted army at a place called Karkor. At this stage Zebah and Zalmunna felt secure and were not expecting Gideon to come so far. Gideon, however, who was a master at the shock tactic, stole up by way of the tent dwellers and attacked the army when they were least expecting it. Gideon focused on the capture of the two kings who were now fleeing for their lives. He kept up a relentless chase until he had captured both Zebah and Zalmunna, throwing the Midianite army into total panic and defeat. The Israelite victory was now complete and Midian, as a military force, was finished at last.

Rather than leading the nation in celebration and thanksgiving, Gideon now wanted to close some unfinished business with his own fellow Israelites. Still stinging with the hurt of rejection, he led his army toward the cities of Succoth and Penuel.

TURNING POINT

We have now reached a turning point in the Book of Judges. Up to this moment the judges have been slaying the enemies of the Lord's people, but now they begin to slay their own brethren. The high mountain peak of the Book of Judges is Gideon's victory over Midian, but this is followed by Israel's gradual descent into internecine strife and division.

Gideon, coming close to the city, captured a young man of Succoth and compelled him to write down the names of the seventy-seven officials and elders of Succoth. On arriving at the city, he was quick to remind the inhabitants that they had taunted him about Zebah and Zalmunna not yet being in his hand. The men of Succoth must have been alarmed to see that the two kings, each on his crescent-decorated camel, were now indeed prisoners of Gideon and his three hundred men. Gideon kept his grisly promise to flail them with thorns and briers. The narrator tells us, "And he took the elders of the city, and thorns of the wilderness and briers, and with them he taught the men of Succoth" (8:16). It was undoubtedly a very cruel form of punishment and one can only imagine the sickening sight of raw flesh and blood as each elder was lacerated with thorns and briers.

This gruesome scene reminds us of an infinitely worse travesty of justice when the Lord Jesus was scourged with a Roman lash across His back. The soldiers twisted thorns into the shape of a crown and mockingly placed it on His head. Taking the reed from His hand, they struck Him on the head and spat in His face. The Son of God knows what it was like to receive cruel and humiliating treatment at the hands of men.

After teaching the men of Succoth a severe lesson, Gideon and his men moved to Penuel. Again, he kept his promise that when he would come in peace, he would break down the tower. That tower would have been the city's defence against its enemies and yet Gideon did not seem to reconsider his vengeful course. Not only did he break down the tower, he also compounded the punishment by slaying his fellow Israelites, "And he tore down the tower of Penuel and killed the men of the city" (8:17). This is a sad, sad turning point in the book of Judges. Instead of uniting the nation, Gideon was prepared to slay his own brethren for the sake of personal vengeance and pride. Doubtless his honour had been wounded, but did he really need to carry out the death penalty on the men of Penuel? Could he not have spared their lives?

Having dealt with the cities of Succoth and Penuel, Gideon now turned his attention to the two kings of Midian and asked, "What kind of men were they whom you killed at Tabor?" It would seem that the brothers of Gideon had been part of a resistance unit hoping to stop the westward advance of the Midianites. Whatever the circumstances, the brothers had fallen into the hands of the Midianites who had shown them no mercy. The kings answered that every one of them resembled Gideon, like the son of a king. Gideon replied, "They were my brothers, the sons of my mother. As the LORD lives, if you had let them live, I would not kill you."

On reading the words of Gideon, one feels like crying out – "O Gideon, have you forgotten? Where are the men you killed at Penuel? Could you not have saved them alive? They were your brethren." What a lesson for every Christian! It is often the case that Christians who will make great sacrifices to win the lost for Christ, will sometimes show great intolerance and rudeness to fellow Christians, often within one's own assembly fellowship. Shame on us!

What happened next does not make particularly pleasant reading. Gideon told Jether his eldest son to rise and kill the kings of Midian. Jether, who was still young, was too frightened to draw his sword. Gideon was asking him to do something for which he was not ready. The kings saw the boy's discomfort and challenged Gideon to carry out the executions himself. Gideon arose and killed both Zebah and Zalmunna, after which, "he took the crescent ornaments that were on their camels' necks" (8:21).

The sequel

Gideon was a man who had great strengths and serious weaknesses. His strength of character was evident in his response to the men of Israel when they made him an offer that lesser men would have found irresistible, "Rule over us, both you and your son, and your grandson also; for you have delivered us from the hand of Midian" (8:22). There is something in human nature that loves power and position. Gideon, to his credit, resisted the temptation and said, "I will not rule over you, nor shall my son rule over you; the LORD shall rule over you." Gideon did not have self-centred ambitions but genuinely desired the LORD's honour and the blessing of His people. What an example for Christian leaders and elders today!

If Gideon had great faith and zeal for the LORD, he was sometimes sadly lacking in wisdom and discernment. What he did next we need have no doubt was done in sincerity. Gideon asked the people to hand over the earrings and ornaments which had been taken as spoil. The narrator informs us that the Midianites wore golden earrings because they were Ishmaelites. There has been a huge revival in our own time of men wearing earrings. Sadly, 'Ishmaelite culture' is often adopted by the LORD's people.

Gideon took the earrings, pendants and crescents and made an image of an ephod which he set up in his home town of Ophrah. Gideon probably thought that this was a noble idea! The man who had destroyed the image of Baal was now replacing it with a golden image of an ephod! Gideon would certainly not be the last man in history to introduce idolatry into worship, though be it unwittingly. The results were truly devastating. The image became a snare to Gideon, to his family, and to all Israel who "played the harlot with it there" (8:27).

Church history is full of examples of idolatry being introduced with the supposed intention of helping people to worship. The leaders of early Christendom argued that images helped the faithful to worship and pray. It was not long until all kinds of relics and objects were being venerated. Pieces of the cross, bones and teeth, crucifixes, images, shrouds and icons have been a snare to countless people down the ages even to our own day. The book of Judges has something important to say to the modern religious world if they would but listen. The story of Gideon and the image of the ephod is an outstanding witness to the folly and danger of idolatry. The apostle John concluded his letter by pleading, "Little children, keep yourselves from idols" (1 John 5:21).

Gideon lived to be an old man and had seventy sons to his many wives. Not content with his wives who presumably lived with him in Ophrah, he also had a concubine in the neighbouring town of Shechem. Gideon's family would reap a bitter harvest from this act of folly.

Gideon's great achievement, under God, was to end Midian's reign of terror in Israel. We read, "Thus Midian was subdued before the children of Israel, so they lifted their heads no more" (8:28). The people of Israel no longer lived in hideouts and caves and could now have normal lives in their own homes, enjoying peace and security. The land had rest for forty years during the life of Gideon. He died an old man and he was buried in his father's tomb in Ophrah of the Abiezrites. And so ended the life of Gideon, a mighty man of valour and a true hero of faith.

After Gideon's death the people once again forgot God. In a shocking display of ingratitude they showed no kindness to the family of Gideon even though he had done such great things for Israel. But, most shocking of all, the people of Israel returned to the worship of Baal. They forsook the God of Abraham, Isaac and Jacob, and in breathtaking unfaithfulness made Baal-berith their god, which means "Baal of the covenant".

The story of Gideon has many lessons to teach us about the will of God, the gospel, and human nature. We have already noted that Midian means strife. Strife between nations can be horrendous; strife between communities can be devastating; strife between brethren is spiritually destructive. To witness an assembly tearing itself apart is heartbreaking. The strife in Corinth prohibited Paul from giving them mature Christian teaching, "And I, brethren, could not speak to you as to spiritual people, but as to carnal, as to babes in Christ. I fed you with milk and not with solid food; for until now you were not able to receive it, and even now you are still not able; for you are still carnal. For where there are envy, strife and divisions among you, are you not carnal and behaving like mere men?" (1 Cor 3:1-3). The strife in the Corinthian church was so bad, and the spiritual condition so carnal, that believers were even taking one another to law.

Ongoing strife will also adversely affect the worship of the local assembly. When Paul turned his attention to the breaking of bread meeting, he had this critical comment to make, "Now in giving these instructions I do not praise you, since you come together not for the better but for the worse. For first of all, when you come together as a church, I hear that there are divisions among you, and in part I believe it ... What shall I say to you? Shall I praise you in this? I do not praise you" (1 Cor 11:17-22). Let us be careful not to behave like Midian in our Christian gatherings.

The story also points us to a greater than Gideon – our Lord Jesus Christ. The strife and enmity which sin brought between man and God has been dealt with on the cross. He has made peace and reconciliation for the sinner on the personal level. That is the message of the gospel that the world needs to hear, a message that will dispel the darkness and bring the light of the knowledge of the glory of God in the face of Jesus Christ.

---

[8] Herzog & Gichon *Battles of the Bible* p.75.

CHAPTER SIX

Judges 9:1-57

Abimelech, the self-appointed Judge

Abimelech is a shocking example of those men who throughout history have been consumed by a lust for power and control. Such people have no scruples about trampling on those who stand in their way and will do anything to have domination over others. Absalom, Herod, Napoleon, Hitler, Stalin and Pol Pot are infamous examples of ruthless and ambitious men who wanted position and power more than anything else. In church life, the same self-promoting spirit can surface in the form of a Diotrephes, the kind of man who wants to rule and control others (3 John 9-10). The desire for power can be either moderate or extreme. Abimelech, our next case study, falls well within the extreme category.

Gideon may have nobly refused the offer of kingship, but he adopted the lifestyle of a self-indulgent king, having multiple wives and children. Not content with his seventy wives, he also had an affair outside of marriage. Gideon fathered an illegitimate son, Abimelech, to a concubine from the nearby town of Shechem. It would seem that the concubine brought Abimelech up in Shechem, while the seventy sons of Gideon, half-brothers to Abimelech, were raised in Ophrah. Abimelech grew up to be one of the most violent and destructive men ever seen in Israel. He was ready to make his move when Gideon died.

Where better to create your powerbase than in the place where you were brought up? Abimelech urged his mother's family to ask the leaders of Shechem whether they would prefer to serve the seventy sons of Jerubbaal or to serve just one leader. He implied that they would be much better off under him, urging them, "Remember that I am your own flesh and bone" (9:2). His mother's relatives successfully persuaded the leaders that Abimelech's proposed seizure of power would be in their best interests. His relatives liked the thought of Abimelech's leadership and responded, "He is our brother."

A take-over of power would require finance and manpower. The funding came from the leaders of Shechem who donated seventy pieces of silver taken from the house of Baal-Berith, money that was undoubtedly earned by idolatry and immorality. Abimelech used the money to hire mercenaries of the worst kind - worthless and reckless fellows. Accompanied by his criminal gang, Abimelech made his way to Ophrah with murder in his heart.

What happened next would rival any Nazi atrocity in its ruthlessness and cruelty. With the help of his hired thugs, Abimelech murdered his seventy brothers in cold blood, all on one stone. The enormity of the crime is truly breathtaking. What Abimelech possibly didn't realise was that Gideon's youngest son, Jotham, had hidden from his brother and had escaped the fratricide.

After he had killed his brothers, Abimelech and his conspirators left the gore-stained stone of Ophrah and made their way to the oak of the pillar at Shechem for the inauguration ceremony. When Abimelech had been declared king and the celebrations were about to begin, the proceedings were interrupted by a man's voice echoing through the air from the slopes of nearby Mount Gerizim. The crowd fell silent as they listened to the voice of Jotham, the youngest son of Gideon and only surviving half-brother of Abimelech.

"Listen to me, you leaders of Shechem, that God may listen to you" cried Jotham loudly. What followed was an indictment of the Shechemites in the form of a fable. The trees, stated Jotham, wanted a king to rule over them. The olive tree, the fig tree and the vine tree each in turn declined the offer of kingship. Finally, all the trees said to the bramble, "You come and reign over us" (9:14). The bramble agreed to be their ruler, while stating that if the offer was in good faith they could take refuge in his shade, but if not, fire would come from the bramble and devour the cedars of Lebanon.

Jotham proceeded to apply the fable and invoke a curse on Abimelech and the men of Shechem and Beth-millo. The idea of a bramble ruling over cedars was utterly perverse. They had chosen Abimelech to rule over them, and had slain the seventy sons of Jerubbaal (Gideon) on one stone. If they have acted in good faith, Jotham said sarcastically, may they rejoice in Abimelech. But if not, may fire come from Abimelech and devour the leaders of Shechem and Beth-millo; likewise, may fire come from Shechem and Beth-millo and devour Abimelech. Having pronounced the curse, Jotham ran for his life in the direction of Beer where he lived in hiding from Abimelech his brother.

There are at least two scriptural references which establish the principle that our choices in life will have predictable consequences. The first is, "God is not mocked, for whatever a man sows, that he will also reap" (Gal 6:7). The second was spoken by the Lord Jesus in the Garden of Gethsemane (alluding to Gen 9:6), "...all who take the sword will perish by the sword" (Matt 26:52). Abimelech and his cohorts were soon to reap the bitter consequences of their actions.

For three troublesome years Abimelech ruled Israel. It was not long until cracks began to appear in the unholy alliance that had wrested power. The narrator tells us that God sent an evil spirit between Abimelech and the leaders of Shechem, "that the violence done to the seventy sons of Jerubbaal might come, and their blood be laid on Abimelech their brother, who killed them, and on the men of Shechem, who strengthened his hand to kill his brothers" (9:23-4).

The killing fields

The men of Shechem received a new leader, a man called

Gaal, the son of Ebed. We read that the people went out to their vineyards in the field and gathered grapes, trampled them, and held a festival. When they went into the house of their god to eat and drink, Gaal reviled Abimelech and his officer Zebul, and bemoaned the fact that he himself was not the leader of the people, "Would that this people were under my hand! Then I would remove Abimelech. I would say to Abimelech, 'Increase your army and come out'" (9:29).

Gaal's challenge to Abimelech's rule soon reached the ears of Zebul. Angered at this threat to his position in Shechem, Zebul secretly sent word to Abimelech to come at night and hide outside the city until morning when he could attack the people as they came out to work in the fields. The next morning there were skirmishes in which Abimelech wounded and chased Gaal and his men right back to the gate of the city. Zebul was then able to drive out Gaal and his relatives from Shechem.

The following day was much worse for fatalities. Again Abimelech set an ambush for the people of Shechem as they worked in the fields, this time dividing his men into three companies. Abimelech's company went and blocked the gates while the other two companies rushed on all the workers in the field and massacred them. We read that Abimelech fought against the city all day and captured it. His fury knew no bounds as he proceeded to kill the people, raze the city and sow it with salt.

There was worse to come. The leaders of the Tower of Shechem, in their fright, took refuge in the stronghold of the house of El-berith. When Abimelech was told that all the leaders were gathered together in the stronghold, he quickly devised a plan that, on a scale of barbarity, was more horrendous than anything else he had done so far. He brought his men to the slopes of Mount Zalmon, took his axe, and cut down a bundle of brushwood. Laying the bundle on his shoulder, he instructed all his men to do the same. They then made their way to the stronghold, piled the brushwood against the building, and set the wood alight. About a thousand men and women were burnt alive in the raging inferno. The first part of Jotham's prophecy was fulfilled - the fire had come out from Abimelech and had consumed the men of Shechem.

Having dealt with Shechem, Abimelech turned his attention on the city of Thebez and encamped against it. On his successful capture of the city, the inhabitants fled to the city tower, shutting themselves in and gathering on the roof. On attacking the tower, Abimelech committed a tactical error which cost him his life. He made the mistake of coming right up to the tower to set fire to the door. This brought him within throwing range of the people on the roof. A woman of the city took the opportunity to drop an upper millstone on Abimelech's head, crushing his skull. As he lay dying he told his armour-bearer to finish him off, lest it should be said of him that a woman had killed him! The servant obliged by ending his master's life, "So his young man thrust him through, and he died" (9:54).

And so the vengeful and violent life of Abimelech ended in suicide. The foot of the tower of Thebez had become, as it were, his 'Berlin bunker' - a tragic ending to a tragic life. When the people saw that Abimelech was dead, they departed to their homes. The narrator informs us, "Thus God repaid the wickedness of Abimelech, which he had done to his father by killing his seventy brothers. And all the evil of the men of Shechem God returned on their own heads, and on them came the curse of Jotham the son of Jerubbaal" (9:56).

There are both military and spiritual lessons to learn from this sad episode. The circumstances of Abimelech's death were to enter the manual of military tactics for future Israelite commanders. It became a maxim of siege warfare not to come within throwing or shooting distance of the walls of a besieged city. This explains Joab's instructions to his messenger as he sent him to tell David of the death of Uriah the Hittite, husband of Bathsheba:

"Then the men of the city came out and fought with Joab. And some of the people of the servants of David fell; and Uriah the Hittite died also. Then Joab sent and told David all the things concerning the war, and charged the messenger, saying, "When you have finished telling the matters of the war to the king, if it happens that the king's wrath rises, and he says to you: 'Why did you approach so near to the city when you fought? Did you not know that they would shoot from the wall? Who struck Abimelech the son of Jerubbesheth? Was it not a woman who cast a piece of a millstone on him from the wall, so that he died in Thebez? Why did you go near the wall?'—then you shall say, 'Your servant Uriah the Hittite is dead also.' "

(2 Sam 11:17-21).

There is certainly spiritual wisdom in this military principle. It is vital for the Christian to keep a safe distance from sin and temptation. In fact, Paul would tell us that there are some things from which the Christian should flee, viz. immorality (1 Cor 6:18); idolatry (1 Cor 10:14); love of money (1 Tim 6:11); and youthful lusts (2 Tim 2:22).

The story of Abimelech, the self-appointed king, also portends a time of trouble which is yet to come on this world. Abimelech was not called of God but was a false judge, an anti-judge. In that sense he resembles the anti-Christ, who will appear at the end of this age. In that day the whole world will follow the beast and the false prophet. Man's current rebellion against God will lead to the ultimate sin – man's self-deification. At that moment, when the man of sin goes into the temple and proclaims himself as God, the great tribulation (spoken of in Matthew 24) will begin against the Jews. The Palestinian, Arab and pan-Islamic hatred for Israel will be unleashed in an unrestrained tidal wave of violence and persecution. When the whole world turns against Israel, "then shall appear the sign of the Son of man in heaven: and then shall all the tribes of the earth mourn, and they shall see the Son of man coming in the clouds of heaven with power and great glory" (Mat 24:30). Just as Abimelech's life was brought to a sudden and violent end, so the man of sin, that latter-day Abimelech, shall be destroyed by the Lord Jesus with the breath of His mouth and the brightness of His coming (2 Thes 2:8).

CHAPTER SEVEN

Judges 10:1-5

Tola and Jair

At this juncture in the history of the nation, the Israelites needed a leader who would not seek his own interests, but those of the Lord's people. Abimelech's reign had been a disaster, bringing strife and division. It was now a time for healing and reconciliation. The country needed strong leadership as never before.

Once again God had His man in the right place, at the right time. We read, "After Abimelech there arose to save Israel Tola..." (10:1). He did not rise to promote himself or to seize power, but to *save Israel*. Not only did Tola save Israel, but he judged the people for no less than twenty-three years.

That would remind us of what Paul said about Timothy, "For I have no one like-minded, who will sincerely care for your state. For all seek their own, not the things which are of Christ Jesus" (Phil 2:20-1). The Lord's people today need men like Tola and Timothy.

We are given the added detail that Tola was of the tribe of Isaachar, but lived in the town of Shamir in the hill country of Ephraim. After twenty-three years of judging Israel, he died and was buried in the town of Shamir. What an excellent epitaph can be written over his life – *he arose to save Israel*.

There is not so much to say about Jair except that he judged Israel for twenty-two years. The narrator gives us no clue as to how faithful or effective he was, but if the events recorded in chapter 10 are in chronological order, the national slide back to idolatry didn't begin until Jair was dead. To his credit, his influence was like that of salt, preserving the nation and delaying its corruption.

We are told that Jair had thirty sons who had thirty donkeys and had thirty cities. The information is given in a rather matter-of-fact fashion, with no comment on the sons' character. One is left with the feeling that the sons of Jair, taking advantage of their father's position, were interested in living a high life. At any rate, the main occupation of their lives seems to have been donkeys and cities. It is not really much of an epitaph. May God deliver us from living mediocre and uncommitted lives.

CHAPTER EIGHT

Judges 10:6 – 12:7

Jephthah,
defender of the inheritance

We have been introduced to several of Israel's enemies in our
journey through the book of Judges. So far, there have been
Mesopotamians, Moabites, Gentiles and Midianites - now it is
the turn of the Ammonites. Half-brothers to the Moabites, they
too were incestuous descendants of Lot by one of his daughters.
They lived in Transjordan, east of the River Jordan, their land
bordering on the territory of Gad. Interestingly, the capital city
of the modern state of Jordan is called Amman, situated in the
old territory of Ammon.

The Ammonites, who worshipped 'the abomination of
Molech', were hateful enemies of Israel. Their strategy was to
encroach on the land of the Israelites and dispossess them of
their God-given heritage. Israel's conflict with the Ammonites
was to do with land and heritage. Ammon speaks of that aspect
of the *world which would rob us of our inheritance.* Jephthah was
prepared to risk his life to defend the inheritance of Israel. But
before considering the complex character of Jephthah, we must
first take a look at the condition of the land and its people.

History was again repeating itself and the lessons of Othniel,
Ehud, Deborah, Barak and Gideon were soon forgotten. When
Tola and Jair died, the people of Israel once again reverted to evil
and idolatry. Their unfaithfulness knew no bounds as they "served
the Baals and the Ashtoreths, the gods of Syria, the gods of Sidon,
the gods of Moab, the gods of the people of Ammon, and the gods

of the Philistines" (10:6). In consequence, the LORD sold the Israelites into the hand of their enemies once again.

The Israelites who lived in Gilead, east of the Jordan, took the brunt of the Ammonite aggression for a period of eighteen years. Not content with staying in Gilead, the Ammonites also crossed the Jordan to harass the tribes of Judah, Benjamin, and Ephraim, so that all Israel was greatly distressed. When the people cried to heaven for deliverance, the response was not what they wanted to hear. The LORD reminded them that He had already delivered them from Egyptians, Amorites, Ammonites, Philistines, Sidonians, Amalekites and Maonites. They had forsaken the LORD and He would save them no more. The LORD mocked the Israelites, "Go and cry out to the gods whom you have chosen; let them deliver you in the time of your distress" (10:14). This taunting challenge would soon reveal the shallowness of the people's confidence in Baal.

Why do people believe a lie and put their trust in something that, deep down in their souls, they know isn't true? When a time of crisis comes, they realise they have been building on sand. The people of Israel, rather belatedly, put away their foreign gods and said to the LORD, "We have sinned! Do to us whatever seems best to You; only deliver us this day, we pray" (10:15). We read of God's stirring response, "And His soul could no longer endure the misery of Israel" (10:16).

The Ammonite army encamped in Gilead in what was a menacing and aggressive show of force. The people of Israel responded by gathering at Mizpah. But Israel had a serious problem – they were leaderless. The chief men of Gilead asked one another, "Who is the man who will begin the fight against the people of Ammon? He shall be head over all the inhabitants of Gilead" (10:18).

Jephthah, the disinherited leader

No person has any responsibility for the circumstances of his or her birth. Some are born into good homes with godly parents, while others begin life in ungodly and dysfunctional homes. Others do not even have a home, but literally live on the streets. In modern times we have the new phenomenon of children being brought up by 'same sex parents', a shocking perversion of family life. Even so, we shall see that God can save and use any man or woman, regardless of a disadvantaged or sinful background.

Jephthah was the son of a prostitute, an unpleasant truth he was never allowed to forget. Gilead, his father, had a wife who bore him sons within his own marriage. When the sons grew up they thrust Jephthah out of the home with words of cruel rejection, "You shall have no inheritance in our father's house, for you are the son of another woman" (11:2). Understandably, Jephthah became an embittered man. He fled to the land of Tob where his leadership qualities were wasted on worthless fellows who were quick to gather around him. The Gileadites, however, soon came to realise that Jephthah was actually the only suitable candidate to defeat the oppressors.

The elders of Gilead had to swallow their pride and go to Jephthah to persuade him to return and lead them against the Ammonites. Jephthah was not long in reminding them of their former treatment of him, "Did you not hate me, and expel me from my father's house? Why have you come to me now when you are in distress?" (11:7). The elders pleaded that it was because of their distress that they now wanted him to return and become head over all Gilead. Jephthah, putting his evident negotiating skills to use, imposed a condition before committing himself, "If you take me back home to fight against the people of Ammon, and the LORD delivers them to me, shall I be your head?" The elders had no option but to accede to Jephthah's demand, "The LORD will be a witness between us, if we do not according to your words." When Jephthah heard that, he returned with the elders of Gilead. The extreme irony of this change in circumstances would not have been lost on Jephthah or the elders.

It has been pointed out by numerous commentators that God did not actually call Jephthah to be a judge. Technically that may be true, but Jephthah was no Abimelech. He had already indicated his belief that if there were to be victory over the Ammonites, it would be the LORD who would give it. Also, when the people made him head over them, we read that "Jephthah spoke all his words before the LORD in Mizpah" (11:11). We shall give Jephthah credit for taking his calling as from the LORD.

Jephthah, now appointed leader, soon proved himself to be an able negotiator. His opening gambit was to send a diplomatic mission to the king of the Ammonites. Adopting a conciliatory tone, Jephthah asked "What do you have against me, that you come to fight against me in my land?" (11:12). The king of the Ammonites told the messengers that Israel, on coming up from Egypt, had stolen land which lay between the River Arnon and the River Jabbock and was bounded by the River Jordan. The king demanded that the disputed territory be returned immediately.

Jephthah did his homework well and became an able defender of Israel's inheritance. He sent messengers for the second time and told the Ammonite king that Israel had not taken any land from the Moabites or the Ammonites. Jephthah explained that when Israel had come out of Egypt, neither the king of Moab nor the king of Edom would allow the people safe passage through their territory. Consequently, Israel had to take a long circuitous route around the land of Moab until they reached the River Arnon. Israel had asked King Sihon for safe passage through his territory. Sihon refused Israel their request and went out to meet them in battle. Jephthah made a bold and uncompromising statement based on the true history of events:

"And the LORD God of Israel delivered Sihon and all his people into the hand of Israel, and they defeated them. Thus Israel gained possession of all the land of the Amorites, who inhabited that country. They took possession of all the territory of the Amorites, from the Arnon to the Jabbok, and from the wilderness to the Jordan. And now the LORD God of Israel has dispossessed the Amorites from before his people Israel; should you then possess it?" (11:21-23)

In summary, the disputed territory from the River Arnon to the River Jabbok and from the wilderness to the River Jordan, had been lost by the Ammonites to the Amorites long before Israel had come out of Egypt.   Israel had taken the territory from the Amorites, not the Ammonites. Jephthah then made a rather derisive proposal, "Will you not possess whatever Chemosh your god gives you to possess? So whatever the LORD our God takes possession of before us, we will possess" (11:24). Jephthah raised the stakes still further by comparing the king of the Ammonites to that other notorious enemy of Israel – Balak the son of Zippor, king of Moab. The Israelites had been living in the disputed territory for no less than three hundred years and Jephthah demanded to know why the Ammonites hadn't recovered the land in all that time.

Jephthah had put his case forcefully by appealing to history. He pleaded not guilty of sinning against the Ammonites, but insisted that the Ammonites were in the wrong to make war against him. The final words that Jephthah's messengers delivered were an appeal for the LORD to judge that day between the Ammonites and the Israelites.

The king of the Ammonites was not interested in discussing the rights and wrongs of his claim to the territory. He didn't want to know about historical facts. He was coveting the territory and he wanted it at any price. The king's reaction is described by the narrator, "However, the king of the people of Ammon did not heed the words which Jephthah sent him" (11:28). The negotiations had come to an end. Jephthah had done his best to achieve peace by diplomacy but that approach had failed. War between Israel and Ammon was now inevitable.

Jephthah, the commander

If there were any doubts that Jephthah was God's choice, we are now reassured by the approving words, "Then the Spirit of the LORD came upon Jephthah..." (11:29). Further, if yet more proof were needed, the inclusion of Jephthah's name in the role of honour in the eleventh chapter of Hebrews surely settles the issue. Jephthah was led by the Spirit as he made his way through Gilead and Manasseh to Mizpah where the army of Israel was waiting. Jephthah and his men were now facing the Ammonite army.

What happened next has become famous in the annals of tragedy. Whether Jephthah was under extreme pre-battle tension we do not know, but he made a rash and foolish vow that he would bitterly regret. He made a bargain with God that he need never have made, saying "If You will indeed deliver the people of Ammon into my hands, then it will be that whatever comes out of the doors of my house to meet me, when I return in peace from the people of Ammon, shall surely be the LORD's, and I will offer it up as a burnt offering" (11:30). It was one thing to promise a votary offering in the event of victory, but it was quite another to sacrifice whatever met him on his return. Having made his vow, Jephthah and his army crossed over to engage the enemy.

The battle was swift and decisive. Jephthah's army advanced like a tidal wave, pushing back the Ammonites from Aroer to Minnith, overrunning twenty cities as far as Abel-keramim. The Ammonites seemed to melt before the Israelites so that the outcome of the action was described as a "very great slaughter". The LORD had given an overwhelming victory to Jephthah. The Ammonites were subdued and the inheritance of the LORD's people was safe.

Jephthah, doubtless elated with victory and thankful to the LORD, made his way back to his dwelling at Mizpah. What should have been an occasion of great family celebration and joy became a horrendous nightmare. As he approached his own home, his daughter came out to greet him with dancing and timbrels. Jephthah's heart sank as he remembered his vow. He was now obliged, in keeping with his promise, to offer his only child as a burnt offering. Tearing his clothes with remorse, He broke the news to his daughter, "Alas, my daughter! You have brought me very low! You are among those who trouble me! For I have given my word to the LORD and I cannot go back on it" (11:35).

Perhaps the most surprising part of this sad drama was his daughter's sense of honour and duty toward her father. She was rejoicing that the LORD had given her father's enemies into his hand, "My father, if you have given your word to the LORD, do to me according to what has gone out of your mouth, because the LORD has avenged you of your enemies, the people of Ammon" (11:36). We do not read of any hint of protest on his daughter's part. Her only request was that she should have two months to wander on the mountains with her friends to bewail her virginity. On her return to her father after two months, the narrator tells us in stark words, "And it was so at the end of two months that she returned to her father, and he carried out his vow with her which he had vowed" (11:39).

These words have perplexed readers for more than two millennia. Did Jephthah literally slay his daughter and offer her as a burnt offering, or did he dedicate her to the LORD in a life of perpetual virginity? As much as we might prefer the latter option, the hard reality seems to point to a literal burnt offering. For an extensive discussion of both sides of the argument, see C.T.Lacey's statement in his commentary on Judges. [9] Commentators who think that Jephthah probably slew his daughter include F.F.Bruce, A.E.Cundall-L.Morris, A.M.S.Gooding, E.J.Hamlin, J.Hercus, Jamieson-Fausset-Brown, W.Kelly, C.T.Lacey and M.Wilcock. Others who think that he did not slay his daughter include A.Clarke, S.J.Robinson, John Wesley and W.W.Wiersbe,

One thing we can be certain about - God never wanted Jephthah to offer his daughter as a burnt offering. Perhaps the whole episode tells us something about the abysmal knowledge of God during the time of the Judges. If Jephthah had inquired into the law of the offerings with the same diligence as he had studied the history of the Ammonites, he would have known the mind of God on the subject of worship and vows. But we cannot be too judgemental on Jephthah, for he had been given a terrible example of faith from his brothers. Cast out of his family as a reject, embittered and criminalised, how could he have any appreciation of the love and holiness of God? It should hardly surprise us that Jephthah held mistaken views about God.

Neglect of the scriptures will take a person's understanding of God further and further from the truth. The medieval Crusades and the later Spanish Inquisition are both notorious examples of unenlightened zeal for God. We need only think of those today who climb sacred mountains barefoot, believing that this will buy them favour with God. But the worst example of misguided zeal in modern times must surely be that of suicide bombers who kill themselves and others, thinking that God will reward them with a sensual paradise The god of the suicide bomber bears terrifying resemblance to Chemosh and Molech, rather than to the living and true God. How deeply thankful we should be to know that the God of the Bible is the God and Father of our Lord Jesus Christ.

What could have saved Jephthah from making his wretched vow? The answer must surely be that Jephthah needed a true, scriptural knowledge of the living God. Such knowledge would also have preserved him from the fratricidal slaughter with which his story ends.

When we come to the New Testament we discover that the Lord Jesus forbids the practice of swearing, "But I say to you, do not swear at all: neither by heaven, for it is God's throne; nor by earth, for it is His footstool; nor by Jerusalem, for it is the city of the great King. Nor shall you swear by your head, because you cannot make one hair white or black. But let your 'Yes' be 'Yes,' and your 'No,' 'No.' For whatever is more than these is of the evil one" (Matt 5:34-37; see also James 5:12).

The Sequel

We have already noted in the earlier story of Gideon that

jealousy and envy are two of the worst human failings. The Ephraimites were jealous at the successes of Gideon and now we find them jealous of Jephthah's victory. They banded together and crossed over the Jordan, demanding to know why Jephthah had not called them to join in the fight with the Ammonites. Their ugly mood quickly became apparent when they added, "We will burn your house down on you with fire!" (12:1). Jephthah replied that when he had called them to help him they had not responded. He had gone to fight the Ammonites without them and God had given them into his hands. Jephthah's final words to the Ephraimites were defiant and unyielding, "Why then have you come up to me this day to fight against me?" (12:3).

What was probably the last straw for Jephthah was the racial and social slur that the Ephraimites made against him and the Gileadites, "You Gileadites are fugitives of Ephraim among the Ephraimites and Manassites" (12:4). This gypsy jibe was too much for Jephthah. He expected insults from enemies like the Ammonites, but he was no longer prepared to be despised by fellow Israelites. Jephthah gathered his army and defeated his brethren the Ephraimites in battle. It would not have been so bad had the violence ended there, but sadly, Jephthah went on slaying after the battle was won.

The circumstances of the post-battle killings are unsurpassed in infamy. The Gileadites knew that the survivors of Ephraim would make their way to the fords of Jordan to cross back into their own land. Pre-empting their action, the Gileadites seized the fords and waited for the Ephraimites to arrive. When an escaped Ephraimite came to the river to pass over, he was asked if he was an Ephraimite. If he denied being of Ephraim, the unfortunate man was then asked to say "Shibboleth". The problem for an Ephraimite was that when he tried to say "Shibboleth" it sounded more like "Sibboleth". He couldn't pronounce it properly. On discovering a man's true identity, the Gileadites slew him in cold blood. The sickening killing went on and on until they had murdered no less than a staggering forty-two thousand of their brethren the Ephraimites.

Jephthah judged Israel for the relatively short period of six years. When he died, he was buried among the cities of Gilead. The dominating theme running through this sad story is that of inheritance. Jephthah was disinherited by his brothers; the Ammonites wanted to disinherit the people of Israel; the Ephraimites wanted to disinherit the Gileadites. There is a very strong analogy in this story with what is happening to our Christian heritage today.

Jephthah, in spite of his disadvantaged background, arose to defend the inheritance of the Lord's people. We should take great courage in this. God can use fallen men and women, saved by grace, to do a work for Him. Whenever we have occasion to defend our heritage of truth, let us do so with grace and wisdom in fellowship with the Lord. For example, we have a heritage in gospel preaching that we should defend at all cost. It is vital to keep to the scriptures and to proclaim the gospel of the grace of God with nothing added. There are those who would want to dethrone grace, and add good works as necessary for salvation. It is a tragedy beyond words when groups who once preached a scriptural gospel sell their heritage, compromising the truth. When it comes to the gospel, there are many modern-day Ammonites who want to disinherit us. May God be pleased to raise up men like Jephthah who, with all his faults, defended the heritage of the Lord's people.

Christianity is now under a sustained attack from the world of unbelief. On the one hand, there are media atheists who claim there is no God and that all life is the result of impersonal forces of time and chance. On the other hand, there are those who espouse a New Age view with a pantheistic creed. Either way, Christianity is mocked and rejected at every level. The current trend in the UK is toward an ever increasing secularisation. Many governments across the world have liberalised sexual laws to such an extent that same sex couples can marry and, worse still, legally adopt children. The governments of the Western world have thrown away their heritage of Christian truth and adopted a world view which could have been that of any Ammonite.

It is not for Christians to try to manipulate the press or media, nor is it for Christians to politicise their activities. In the view of this author, the correct strategy for believers in the twenty-first century is to put on the whole armour of God, to pray in the Spirit and to go out preaching the gospel of peace to all. The Christian's only offensive weapon is the sword of the Spirit which is the word of God (Eph 6:17).

Before concluding our thoughts, we must consider the two sad lessons in the story of Jephthah. They both concern his relations with his family and brethren. Firstly, his rash vow meant that his daughter was offered as a burnt offering. That was never the will of God for Jephthah's daughter. It is a very sad thing if our view of God is so twisted and perverse that we allow our actions to harm our loved ones. Secondly, we shudder at the appalling spectacle of Jephthah slaying his brethren the Ephraimites. How often do Christians misdirect their energy and, instead of concentrating on gospel activity, put their time and effort into attacking their own brethren. Indeed, we sometimes slay our brothers, not because they are doctrinally wrong, but because they pronounce 'Shibboleth' differently. Shame on us! May God grant us to love one another so that the world will know that we are truly the Lord's disciples.

---

[9] Lacey C.T. *Judges* in "Joshua, Judges, Ruth" of *What the Bible Teaches* series (Ritchie Old Testament Commentaries, Kilmarnock, Scotland, 2006) pp.382-6.

CHAPTER NINE

Judges 12:8-15

Ibzan, Elon and Abdon

Sometimes in the Old Testament we are expressly told whether a person's life was good or evil. For example, the kings of Judah and Israel are normally described as having done that which was right in the eyes of the Lord, or alternatively having done that which was evil. However, it is also a feature of the Old Testament that a person's life and actions are often recorded without any kind of appraisal or comment, leaving the reader to ponder on the moral and spiritual implications. Such is the situation in the case of the three minor judges: Ibzan, Elon and Abdon.

Ibzan, whose name means *splendid* or *active*, came from Bethlehem. That would certainly remind us of One who was born in Bethlehem and was gloriously splendid and who came to do a work which would be eternal in its consequences. Ibzan arranged marriages for his thirty sons and thirty daughters. After judging Israel for seven years, Ibzan died and was buried in Bethlehem.

Even less is known about Elon the Zebulonite, who judged Israel ten years and was buried in Aijalon. The name Elon means *an oak* or *strong*. We do not know any details of Elon's achievements or actions, but it is comforting to think that for at least ten years the people had a God-appointed leader whose name spoke of strength. Similarly, the Lord's people today need strong leadership more than ever.

Finally, we come to the strange case of Abdon, whose name means *service* or *cloud of judgement*. Abdon came from Pirathon in the land of Ephraim and judged Israel for eight years. His judgement in personal and family matters seems to have been rather clouded. He had forty sons and thirty nephews, providing them with a total of seventy ass colts. It would appear that Abdon had indulged himself with a plurality of wives, and had indulged his family with the trappings of wealth.

In Christian service it is essential that we do not abuse our liberty or rights by taking advantage of the generosity of the Lord's people. Paul reminded the Thessalonians, "For you yourselves know how you ought to follow us, for we were not disorderly among you; nor did we eat anyone's bread free of charge, but worked with labour and toil night and day, that we might not be a burden to any of you, not because we do not have authority, but to make ourselves an example of how you should follow us" (2 Thess 3:7-9).

CHAPTER TEN

Judges 13:1 – 16:31

Samson, the reluctant Nazirite

Samson is one of the most enigmatic characters of our Bible. On the one hand, his exploits of strength and heroism have secured him a place in the great gallery of faith in Hebrews 11; on the other hand, his failures and excesses stand as stark warnings to all generations. As we shall presently see, Samson was "a strange mixture of spirit and flesh."[10]

The Israelites' cyclical lapse into evil had repeated itself another time and the people had again forsaken the living God for the abomination of Baal. As a result, the LORD delivered them into the hand of the Philistines for a period of 40 years. It is alarming how quickly a generation can forget God and embrace idolatry. In our own day and age, it is equally frightening to watch the rapid secularisation of modern UK society. The rising generation of teens and twenties, for the most part, has little more than a receding memory of Christianity.

Strangely, we do not read of the Israelites crying to God for deliverance on this occasion. Perhaps they had sunk so low that they no longer had a moral and spiritual sense of need. A faithless generation had imbibed a Philistine worldview, while the Law of Moses and the covenants had faded out of the national consciousness and into folk memory. God had not only to save His people from the Philistines; He had to save them from themselves. And yet the LORD had not forgotten His people Israel. He would once again provide a deliverer, a man set apart for service from his mother's womb. Like all good biographies, the story begins with the parents.

Manoah and his wife

In Bible times, a childless marriage was the cause of bitter disappointment and the occasion of much heart-searching. Children were considered to be a blessing from God, while infertility was looked on as a sign of God's displeasure. Although Manoah's wife was barren, God had plans for them which they never could have foreseen.

Manoah, a member of the tribe of Dan, lived in the town of Zorah which was located to the west of Jerusalem and close to Philistine territory. On one eventful day the Angel of the LORD appeared to Manoah's wife and said, "Indeed now, you are barren and have borne no children, but you shall conceive and bear a son" (13:3). The Angel continued with strict stipulations regarding the child's upbringing in preparation for his vocation and service. Her son would begin to deliver Israel from the Philistines.

One of the most sacred trusts that God gives to any married couple is to bring a child into the world and to raise it for Him. Every Christian parent should be deeply conscious of the privilege of bringing up their family for God. Manoah's wife was given an extra special commission in that this child was to be a Nazirite to God from the womb. So what exactly was a Nazirite and how would this impact on his upbringing?

Normally, the Law of the Nazirite outlined in Numbers 6, applied to men or women who chose to consecrate themselves to God for a specified period of time. However, there were also special cases in scripture when God marked men out as Nazirites from their mother's womb until the day of their death. The three famous Nazirites of the Bible, namely Samson, Samuel and John the Baptist, were each separated unto God from the womb.

There were three main obligations in the law of the Nazirite:

1) He/she was to drink or eat nothing which came from the grapevine. This meant he was not to drink wine, or wine

vinegar, or even grape juice. Neither was he to eat fresh grapes or raisins.

2) During the days of his vow he was not to cut his hair or to let a razor come near his head. His hair was to be allowed to grow untrimmed.

3) The Nazirite was not to go near a dead body, not even for his father or mother, brother or sister.

Manoah's wife was told to refrain from alcoholic drink while she was expecting Samson, "Now therefore, please be careful not to drink wine or similar drink, and not to eat anything unclean. For behold, you shall conceive and bear a son. And no razor shall come upon his head, for the child shall be a Nazirite to God from the womb; and he shall begin to deliver Israel out of the hand of the Philistines" (13:4-5).

The woman found her husband and told him about the man who had spoken to her. She did not know his name, or where he was from, but she described him as a Man of God "like the Angel of God, very awesome" (13:6). The woman informed her husband of all that the Angel of God had said.

Manoah appeared to be somewhat incredulous at his wife's words and prayed to the LORD that the Man of God might return to teach them what they must do for this special child. God listened to the voice of Manoah and answered his prayer. The Angel of God returned and appeared to Manoah's wife while she was sitting in the field. She immediately rushed to find her husband and advised him that the Man who had appeared to her a few days earlier was back again. Manoah arose and followed his wife to the field where the Man was waiting.

"Are you the Man who spoke to this woman?" asked Manoah. When the Man had answered in the affirmative, Manoah said, "Now let your words come to pass! What will be the boy's rule of life, and his work?" (13:12). The Angel of the LORD repeated the commandment He had already given to the woman, warning again that she was not to eat or drink anything that came from the vine or was unclean. The Angel charged Manoah concerning his wife, "All that I commanded her let her observe" (13:14). When Manoah invited the Angel of the LORD to wait and eat with them, the Angel replied that He would not eat any food, but that Manoah should offer a burnt offering to the LORD. It is at this point in the narrative we learn that Manoah had still not realised he was speaking to the Angel of the LORD. When he enquired after the visitor's name, the Angel of the LORD replied, "Why do you ask My name, seeing it is wonderful?" (13:18).

What happened next must have been a complete shock to Manoah and his wife. When Manoah offered the young goat and the grain offering on a rock to the LORD, he and his wife watched with astonishment as the Man ascended in the flame toward heaven. Overwhelmed and traumatised, Manoah and his wife fell on their faces to the ground. They now realised that He was none other than the Angel of the LORD.

In some marriages, as in Manoah's, the wife can be more spiritually discerning than the husband. On realizing that they had been visited by the Angel of the LORD, Manoah lamented to his wife, "We shall surely die, because we have seen God" (13:22). The woman's reply is a deeply insightful observation on the faithful and gracious character of God,

"If the LORD had desired to kill us, He would not have accepted a burnt offering and a grain offering from our hands, nor would He have shown us all these things, nor would He have told us such things as these at this time" (13:23)

This is a good time to pause and reflect. Some Christians are plagued with doubts about their personal salvation and instead of resting on the value of Christ's sacrifice, they agonise over whether God has really saved them. Such people normally have no doubts about the person of Christ or His ability to save, but are unsure about their own conversion experience. Manoah seems to have been a doubter like that, but his wife had no such problem. She appreciated that God had accepted a sacrifice from their hands and that He had shared His plans and purposes with them. Why would the LORD have done such things had He meant to do them harm? Manoah's wife knew that God's intentions toward them were entirely gracious and she strengthened her husband in his faith.

Sometimes, as Christians, we too need that kind of re-assurance. God has accepted Christ's sacrifice on our behalf, and has made known His purposes toward us. Would He have done such things if He had intended to reject us? Let us be strong in the Lord and share our certainties with others, for by so doing we will help to strengthen the weak.

In due time, the Angel's promise came true and the woman bore a son and called him Samson. The narrator adds the beautiful words, "and the child grew, and the LORD blessed him" (13:24). We read that the Spirit of the LORD began to move upon him at a place called Mahaneh Dan between Zorah and Eshtaol.

Fatal attraction

Samson was attracted to unconverted Philistine women, a weakness that he was never to overcome. We read of three women in his life – first, a Philistine woman from Timnah who became his wife; second, a casual encounter with a Philistine prostitute in Gaza; and third, a Philistine woman named Delilah, who betrayed him.

Samson put his own desires before the interests of his family, his nation and his God. Ideally, Samson should have been looking for a godly Hebrew wife who would have been a help to him in his service for God. It would seem, however, that he found the looks of the Philistine women to be more alluring than those of the Hebrew women. He made his choices by appearance rather than by character, by looks rather than by godliness. When Samson eyed a Philistine woman in Timnah, he immediately informed his father and mother that he wanted her as his wife. "I have seen a woman in Timnah of the daughters of the Philistines" he said, "now therefore, get her for me as a wife" (14:2).

Samson's parents tried to dissuade him from taking a wife from the idol-worshipping Philistines. They were inveterate enemies of Israel and had no part in God's covenants and promises, hence the emphasis on their being "uncircumcised". Samson showed no interest in his parents' concerns and insisted on having his own way, "Get her for me, for she pleases me well." At the core of Samson's thinking was himself; his favourite word was *"me"*. Reluctantly, Samson's parents accompanied him to Timnah to negotiate the marriage.

There are times, in the ways of God, when the Lord's hand is hidden from view and His actions are not immediately discernible. This was such a time. God, who was allowing Samson to make his own selfish choices, was planning to overrule and act in judgement against the Philistines (14:4). His parents did not know that it was of the LORD.

We are told that the family group came to the vineyards of Timnah. Normally, such a piece of information would be of no real consequence, merely something to identify the location. However, in this case it had a rather ominous significance. Samson, as a Nazirite, was to have no contact with the vine or its produce. Samson was not only taking a wife from among the daughters of the uncircumcised Philistines, but he was taking her from a town known for its vineyards.

Samson was typical of the believer who lives as close to the world as possible. There are many things in life that are not actually unlawful for the Christian, but will not help his or her spiritual growth in any way. Paul elaborated on this principle to the Corinthians by writing, "All things are lawful for me, but not all things are helpful" (1 Cor10:23).

On his arrival in Timnah, Samson was taken by surprise by an aggressive young lion. There is probably nothing in life that could be more terrifying than being attacked suddenly by a roaring lion. Normally, an unarmed man would stand no chance in such an unequal contest of strength, but it is recorded that "the Spirit of the LORD came mightily upon him, and he tore the lion apart as one would have torn apart a young goat, though he had nothing in his hand" (14:6). We might well wonder if Samson fully appreciated the superhuman strength with which God had empowered him. He had the potential to be one of Israel's greatest deliverers. Sadly, although listed as a man of faith, Samson never rose to his full God-given potential. Perhaps few of us ever do!

Samson's physical contact with the carcass of the slain lion would necessarily have required a prescribed cleansing ceremony (see Num 6:9-12). Interestingly, Samson did not tell his parents. When he finally met with the Philistine woman and talked to her, she pleased him well.

After an interval of time Samson returned to take the woman as his wife. On his way, curiosity compelled him to turn aside and look at the carcass of the lion that he had killed earlier. This morbid interest in a dead body, as we have already noted, went against the law of the Nazarite. He should not have approached it or touched it, and yet out of this corrupting carcass he found something that appealed to his taste. What a striking picture of sin, which offers to man something that appeals to his fallen nature, but eventually pays the wages of death. On discovering that a swarm of bees and honey were in the carcass, he took some with his hands and went on his way eating it. He also gave some of the honey to his father and mother without telling them that he had taken it from the carcass of a dead animal. Samson obviously had a bad conscience about his own unfaithfulness and felt obliged to keep it secret from his parents. Disobedience in the life of a believer not only defiles the person, but also has a negative effect on fellowship with other believers. The Christian should stay well away from anything remotely sinful, no matter how much it might appeal to his natural taste.

What followed was a wedding ceremony that was bizarre in the extreme. Samson, in accordance with custom, gave a feast which lasted seven days. One can only guess at the amount of wine that would have been consumed at a week long banquet. A Philistine wedding would not have been a healthy place for a Nazirite! On this occasion, the bride's guests would presumably have outnumbered the groom's, and so Samson was given thirty companions from the city.

Samson then posed a riddle to his thirty Philistine groomsmen. If they solved the riddle he would provide them with thirty linen garments and changes of clothing; but if they failed, they must provide the same to him. They took up the challenge and Samson put the riddle to them:

"Out of the eater came something to eat,
And out of the strong came something sweet."

Practical jokes can sometimes go seriously wrong. Samson's wife had been trying for seven days to persuade him to disclose the meaning of the riddle. The Philistines, who were baffled by the puzzle, threatened to burn Samson's wife and her father's house with fire if she did not tell them the answer before the time was up. The woman turned on the tears and pleaded with Samson, "You only hate me! You do not love me! You have put a riddle to the sons of my people, but you have not explained it to me" (14:16). The use of the word 'love' by his wife was about as meaningful as its use in modern popular songs.

Eventually, on the seventh day, Samson could no longer resist the pleading of his wife and divulged the key to the riddle. She immediately passed on the answer to the men of the city who in turn announced it to Samson before the sun went down: "What is sweeter than honey? And what is stronger than a lion?" (14:18).

This was a moment of disillusionment for Samson. He realised his wife had betrayed his trust under pressure from the men of the city. He expressed his anger in his customary cryptic manner:

> *"If you had not plowed with my heifer,*
> *You would not have solved my riddle."*

Samson kept his side of the bargain, but not in a way the Philistines were expecting. The Spirit of the LORD came upon Samson mightily and he made his way to Ashkelon where he killed thirty men, took their garments, and duly gave them to the companions to whom he had posed the riddle.

The marriage was a short one by any standard. Samson, in his anger, left his wife and returned to his father's house. His wife was then given by her father to the companion who had been his best man. After some time Samson felt the urge to return to his wife. It was at the time of wheat harvest when, arriving with the gift of a goat, he told his father-in-law that he wanted to go into his wife's room. Her father would not permit Samson to enter and instead offered her younger sister to him.

If Samson had any previous qualms about harming Philistines, he definitely had none now. "This time I shall be blameless regarding the Philistines if I harm them" he told them. He then caught a staggering three hundred foxes, tied them in pairs with torches attached to their tails, and let them into the wheat harvest to spread fire. The destruction was devastating; the fires destroyed the shocks and standing grain, as well as the vineyards and the olive groves. When the Philistines discovered that Samson was responsible, they murdered both his wife and her father by burning them with fire. Samson was enraged and took his revenge by attacking the Philistines with "a great slaughter" (15:8).

Ungrateful brethren

Samson had the bitter experience of being betrayed by his Philistine wife, but now he was to know the feeling of rejection by his own countrymen. The Philistines, who were seeking revenge against Samson, came up and encamped against Lehi. When the men of Judah demanded to know why the Philistines had deployed themselves against them, they were told that the object of the manoeuvres was to arrest Samson "to do to him as he has done to us" (15:10). To avoid a confrontation with the Philistines, the Israelites went to the rock of Etam to take Samson and hand him over to his enemies.

It is evident that the men of Judah had no appreciation of Samson and his ability to deliver them from the Philistines. Three thousand of the men of Judah went to the cleft of the rock of Etam and demanded of Samson, "Do you not know that the Philistines rule over us? What is this you have done to us?" (15:11). The people had lost the moral and spiritual fibre to resist Philistine rule. They had forgotten that they were a redeemed people, separated to God for service and worship. They were comfortable in their slavery. Sadly, in modern times, Christians can easily forget that they too are a redeemed and separated people. Have we become comfortable in an ungodly "uncircumcised" world?

After promising Samson that they would not kill him, the three thousand men arrested him, bound him with new ropes, and brought him to the Philistines at Lehi. It would not be the last time that the nation of Israel would betray its Deliverer into the hands of Gentile sinners. When the Philistines saw Samson bound they were delirious with glee and came forward shouting against him. What followed was a dramatic demonstration of the power of God over His people's enemies. The narrator tells us, "Then the Spirit of the LORD came mightily upon him; and the ropes that were on his arms became like flax that is burned with fire, and his bonds broke loose from his hands" (15:14). Samson found the jawbone of an ass and used it as a weapon to kill a thousand Philistines. What a terrifying sight it must have been for any onlooker to watch this long-haired Hebrew wielding the jawbone with superhuman strength and felling Philistine after Philistine.

When the killing was over, Samson surveyed the heaps of bodies and recited a victory poem:

> *With the jawbone of a donkey,*
> *Heaps upon heaps,*

*With the jawbone of a donkey
I have slain a thousand men*

The sheer physical exertion of such a colossal task had made Samson very thirsty. He threw down the jawbone and began to pray, "You have given this great deliverance by the hand of Your servant; and now shall I die of thirst and fall into the hand of the uncircumcised?" (15:18). Samson knew that it was foreign to the character of God to deliver someone only to see him fall. When God saves us, He does not forsake us; and when we pray to Him, He hears us: "Now this is the confidence that we have in Him, that if we ask anything according to His will, He hears us" (1 John 5:14).

God heard Samson's prayer and answered by splitting the hollow place in Lehi. The water came out and Samson drank. We read the encouraging words, "...he drank; and his spirit returned, and he revived" (15:19). There are times when a Christian, weary with service, needs to rest awhile, drink of the 'living water' and be revived. Samson aptly named the place En Hakkore, which means *Spring of the Caller*. May we all resort there often!

We are told that Samson "...judged Israel twenty years in the days of the Philistines" (15:20). It was never going to be easy to lead the Lord's people in such an alien culture as the Philistines were ungodly, aggressive and cruel. Likewise, each of us must serve our own generation. There are Christians in the world who live in fear for their lives. Those of us in the West are alarmed at the relentless ongoing secularisation of society as we see our culture becoming more and more Philistine. We in the West should be praying earnestly for believers in the Middle East and Far East where life for Christians can be extremely dangerous.

Samson at his weakest

What follows in the narrative leaves us with a lingering question: Is this incident an example of Samson at his weakest or at his worst? Samson, apparently alone, goes into the Philistine city of Gaza. That was surely a mistake to begin with. Whether he had gone to Gaza with sin on his mind, or had strayed into the path of unexpected temptation, is hard to judge. Either way, when a man finds himself alone in the company of the ungodly, he becomes dangerously vulnerable to sin and temptation.

We read that Samson "saw a harlot there, and went in to her" (16:1). It would seem that Samson had very little self-control in this area of his life. He saw the harlot and that was enough to tempt him. If only Samson had followed the example of Joseph before him and fled from temptation. We need to be careful what we look at, be it in the form of media, press or internet images. The Bible tells us to "Flee sexual immorality" (1 Cor 6:18). What a warning for Christians today!

When the men of Gaza realised that Samson was in their city, they waited for him in silence at the city gate, planning to kill him in the morning. Samson outwitted them by leaving at midnight and, in another outstanding demonstration of physical strength, lifted the gates, posts and bars on to his shoulders and literally walked away with them. He carried them to the top of the hill which overlooked Hebron and there he deposited them. We are not told the reaction of the men of Gaza, nor indeed that of the men of Hebron. They could not have failed to realise that a mighty man was among them. What a pity that his physical strength was not matched by his moral strength!

Samson and Delilah

Samson fell in love yet again, this time with a woman whose name will forever be associated with treachery and unfaithfulness. The lords of the Philistines came to Delilah and offered her a huge bribe of eleven hundred pieces of silver if she would betray the secret of Samson's strength. Delilah did not seem to have any qualms as she set about her covert task.

By comparison, we can only marvel at the paltry sum of thirty pieces of silver that was given by the rulers of Israel to Judas Iscariot for the betrayal of the Lord Jesus. What a low value they placed on their Messiah and King!

Three times Samson lied to Delilah about the secret of his strength. He first told her that if he were tied with seven fresh bowstrings, he would become weak like any other man. Secondly, he stated that if he were bound securely with new ropes, he would become weak. Thirdly, he advised her that if his seven locks of hair were woven into the web of a loom, he would lose his strength. On each occasion, Delilah arranged for Philistines to be waiting in another room so that they could overpower and bind him. To their frustration, Samson broke the bowstrings as a strand of yarn breaks when it touches fire; he snapped the new ropes like thread; and he easily pulled out the batten and web from the loom. Delilah realised that Samson had been mocking her every time.

Delilah, however, was a manipulative woman and knew how to wear down Samson's resistance. She pleaded, "How can you say 'I love you,' when your heart is not with me? You have mocked me these three times, and have not told me where your great strength lies" (16:15). Samson listened to her coaxing day after day until he could resist no longer. He could kill a thousand men with the jawbone of an ass, but he could not withstand the wiles of a seductress. In the end Samson told her everything: he had been a Nazirite unto God from his mother's womb; no razor had ever come on his head; and if his head were shaven, he would become weak like any other man. The God-appointed Judge of Israel had foolishly shared holy things with an ungodly and faithless woman, a daughter of the uncircumcised Philistines.

Delilah knew intuitively that this time Samson had told her the truth. She wasted no time in arranging for the Philistines to come to the house. She lulled him to sleep on her knees and called for a man to cut his hair. Quickly and quietly the man shaved the seven locks of his hair, doubtlessly taking great care not to waken Samson. When his hair was cropped short, Delilah began to taunt him, "Samson, the Philistines are upon you!" (16:20).

This portrays a sad picture of spiritual apathy and carelessness. Samson was asleep when all around lurked treachery and betrayal. What a lesson for Christians today! Have we fallen asleep while dangers are all around us? Paul exhorted the Roman believers, "...now it is high time to awake out of sleep; for now our salvation is nearer than when we first believed" (Rom 13:11).

Samson awoke from sleep and thought that he could rise and defeat the Philistines as before, but he did not know that the LORD had left him. The Philistines seized Samson, gouged out his eyes and bound him in fetters, taking him to prison to grind for his enemies. This is one of the saddest scenes in our Bible. Samson, who could have been a mighty man of God, was now a blind and defeated prisoner of the uncircumcised Philistines. The poet John Milton captured the pathos in these words:

> *Ask for this great deliverer now, and find him*
> *Eyeless in Gaza at the mill with slaves*

Milton, from *"Samson and Agonistes"*

How sad when a Christian ends his life blind and defeated. The scriptures exhort us not to lose our vision. The Lord wrote to the church of the Laodiceans,

"Because you say, 'I am rich, have become wealthy, and have need of nothing' – and do not know that you are wretched, miserable, poor, blind, and naked – I counsel you to buy from Me gold refined in the fire, that you may be rich; and white garments, that you may be clothed, that the shame of your nakedness may not be revealed; and anoint your eyes with eye salve, that you may see" (Rev 3:17-18)

While Samson was in prison, his hair began to grow again and his strength to return. This is very encouraging for the believer who has experienced defeat or failure in his life. God can still use us, even after we have failed Him. The great New Testament example of service after failure is Peter. Let us take courage and make sure that as we grow older, we do not lose our vision. May the Lord open our eyes to realise that He that is in us is greater than he that is in the world (1 John 4:4).

The world celebrates when a Christian falls. The Press and Media love to expose secret sin or unfaithfulness in the lives of professing Christians, especially if they have a public profile. We should remember that the world has no love for the believer. The Lord Jesus said to His disciples, "If the world hates you, you know that it hated me before it hated you" (John 15:18). The world loves to see a Christian's testimony in ruins.

The Philistines were no different in this respect. They rejoiced to see Samson enslaved and humiliated - living proof, so they thought, that their god Dagon was stronger than the God of the Israelites. It was now time to gloat. They organised a great celebration in the temple of Dagon and brought Samson from the prison to mock him. Three thousand Philistines cheered and jeered as a lad led Samson by the hand into the temple. They praised their god for a great deliverance:

> *"Our god has delivered into our hands our enemy,*
> *The destroyer of our land,*
> *And the one who multiplied our dead."*

(16:24)

The spectators, both men and women, continued to scoff and mock as Samson was made to perform for their amusement. On being located between the two supporting pillars of the temple, he asked the lad who held his hand to let him feel the pillars. Then Samson called to the Lord for the last time:

> *"O Lord God, remember me, I pray, just this once, O God,*
> *that I may with one blow take vengeance on the Philistines for my*
> *two eyes!"*

(16:28)

God remembered Samson and answered his prayer in a most

spectacular way. With supernatural strength, Samson heaved on the two pillars with all his might until the temple structure began to totter and collapse. The whole building was soon crashing to the ground in ruins, crushing and burying the Philistine revellers. When the dust had settled, relatives searched in vain for survivors. The idol of Dagon was shattered and broken, while Samson lay dead among the Philistines. The narrator informs us that, "the dead he killed in his death were more than he had killed in his life" (16:30).

In his last hours, Samson was blind and alone as he endured the mockery and taunting of his Philistine captors. We see a parallel when we read of the last hours of the Lord Jesus and discover that His own people blindfolded Him, while mocking and punching Him. They added insult to injury by spitting in His face. When the Jews had done their worst, they handed over their unwanted King to the Roman authorities. It was now the turn of the Roman soldiers to indulge in spitting, mocking and punching. They also crowned Him with thorns and scourged Him. The mockery continued right to the cross, where the chief priests, scribes and Roman soldiers gloated in Christ's apparent defeat. The Lord Jesus suffered for six hours while nailed to the cross. During the second three hours, darkness descended across the whole earth until Christ had finished His work. He dismissed His spirit in death. Like Samson, He accomplished more in His death than in His life.

Had the Lord Jesus not died on the cross, not one single sin could have been forgiven, and not one sinner could have been saved. His death ushered in a new era of grace in God's dealings with the human race. When news was brought to the Lord Jesus that some Greeks wanted to see Him, the Lord spoke of a sea change to come: "And I, if I am lifted up from the earth, will draw all peoples to Myself" (John 12:32).

But what exactly did Christ do on the cross? This important question is best answered in the words of Scripture. The Bible describes Christ's work on the cross in a number of different terms, for example: He gave His life as a ransom for many (Mk 10:45); He died for our sins (1 Cor 15:3); He died for us (Rom 5:8); He died for the ungodly (Rom 5:6); He reconciled us to God (Rom 5:10); He was delivered up for us all (Rom 8:32); He gave Himself for our sins (Gal 1:4); He gave Himself for me (Gal 2:20); He redeemed us from the curse of the law (Gal 3:13); He secured redemption through His blood (Col 1:14); He reconciled all things to God (Col 1:20); He made peace by the blood of His cross (Gal 1:20); He gave Himself a ransom for all (1 Tim 2:6); He purged our sins (Heb 1:3); He tasted death for everyone (Heb 2:9); He destroyed him that had the power of death, that is, the devil (Heb 2:14); He obtained eternal redemption (Heb 9:12); He offered Himself without spot to God (Heb 9:14); He put away sin by the sacrifice of Himself (Heb 9:26); He bore the sins of many (Heb 9:28); He offered one sacrifice for sins forever (Heb 10:12); He redeemed us by His blood (1 Pet 1:18-19); He bore our sins in His own body (1 Pet 2:24); He suffered once for sins (1 Pet 3:18); He became the propitiation for our sins, and not for ours only but also for the whole world (1 John 2:2). What a Saviour!

Samson's service is summarised in the words, "He had judged Israel twenty years" (16:31). What conflicting thoughts must have gone through the minds of Samson's brothers as they came down to Gaza to retrieve the body for burial in his father Manoah's tomb. As they laid the body of the great man to rest, did they wonder what might have been? Samson's ministry, however, pales into insignificance when compared to that of Christ. In His death, the Lord Jesus settled the whole sin question, not for twenty years, but for eternity. The body of Samson has long since returned to dust; yet when two faithful followers of Christ reverently laid the body of Jesus in a garden tomb, little did they realise that in three days He would rise again having defeated the greatest enemy of all - death itself.

It need not be stated that today Samson can save no one. There would be absolutely no point in calling on Samson to save us. By glorious contrast, the Bible exhorts us to call on the risen and living Lord Jesus Christ to save us, "For whoever calls on the name of the Lord shall be saved" (Rom 10:13). Let us make sure that we have called on Him who is the Saviour of the world.

We have already noted in the story of Shamgar that the *'uncircumcised' Philistines speak of human religion in its uncleanness and alienation from God.* The Christian today must separate from all that is false, unclean and 'Philistine'. The story of Samson highlights the danger of the unequal yoke, a subject which Paul takes up in his second letter to the Corinthians:

"Do not be unequally yoked together with unbelievers. For what fellowship has righteousness with lawlessness? And what communion has light with darkness? And what accord has Christ with Belial? Or what part has a believer with an unbeliever? And what agreement has the temple of God with idols? ...Come out from among them and be separate, says the LORD. Do not touch what is unclean, and I will receive you"
(2 Cor 6:14-17).

We end our case study of Samson by recalling that his name is written in the book of Hebrews as a man of faith, along with Gideon, Barak and Jephthah (Heb 11:32). Perhaps, if the decision had been ours, we would not have included Samson's name, writing him off as we sometimes do with other Christians, downgrading them in our judgement to be of no consequence. And yet God, the Judge of all, has included Samson in His great honours list of faith. That is tremendously encouraging. Let us keep on doing what we can, though it be in weakness, to please our Lord and Saviour, Jesus Christ.

---

[10] I recall hearing this striking description used by the late Jack Hunter of Kilmarnock during one of his memorable platform character studies.

CHAPTER ELEVEN

Judges 17:1 – 18:31

Micah and his gods

One of the most dangerous mistakes in religious life is to mix truth with error. A little bit of truth can give credibility to a religious system which is rotten at the core. The people of Israel fell into this trap by mixing the Law of Moses with Baal worship. Indeed, it would seem that idolatry had gradually become endemic throughout Israel. They had entirely forgotten Joshua's last words to their fathers, "Now therefore, put away the foreign gods which are among you, and incline your heart to the Lord God of Israel" (Jos 24:23).

A man named Micah, from the mountains of Ephraim, had stolen eleven hundred shekels of silver from his mother. He later had a change of heart, confessed the theft to his mother and returned the sum in full. The woman, who had invoked a curse on the thief, then relented, blessing her son in the name of the LORD. Highly relieved that the lost money had reappeared, Micah's mother told him what she had originally intended to do with it, "I had wholly dedicated the silver from my hand to the LORD for my son, to make a carved image and a moulded image; now therefore, I will return it to you" (17:3). She gave two hundred shekels of the money to a silversmith to make the two images which she then presented to Micah. How profoundly sad that a 'mother in Israel' should contribute to her son's household collection of idols.

Not only did Micah have a shrine, an ephod and idols in his home, but he compounded the sin by appointing his own son as a priest. The ignorance of scripture had reached a dangerous new low. The laws concerning priesthood as given to Israel through Moses were no longer practised within the nation. The religious and social outlook of the people is described in the rather terse words, "In those days there was no king in Israel; everyone did what was right in his own eyes" (17:6).

At that time there was a young Levite who had left his home in Bethlehem and was wandering through the mountains of Ephraim looking for employment as a priest. His journey led him to the house of Micah where his occupation was soon discovered in conversation. Micah offered the young man the post of family priest for an annual income of ten shekels of silver, along with a suit of clothes, his food and keep. The young man accepted the offer and became his consecrated priest. The mentality of Micah is revealed in his own words, "Now I know that the LORD will be good to me, since I have a Levite for a priest!" (17:13). For Micah, having a Levite as a priest was little more than a good luck charm. He would not be the last to regard religion as a means to an end. Countless kings and leaders throughout history, both in war and peace, have paid religious clerics to look after their spiritual needs and so ensure the blessing and favour of their particular deity or saint. It was perhaps understandable that pagans should practise such empty rituals, but it becomes a serious travesty of truth when professing Christians stoop to such self-serving lies. The history of Christendom is thoroughly corrupted with the spirit and mentality of Micah.

The narrator, having again reminded us that, "In those days there was no king in Israel" (18:1), now moves the story into its second phase. There were five men from the tribe of Dan who arrived and lodged in the house of Micah. On hearing the voice of the young Levite, they recognised him and asked what he was doing and how he had come to be there. The young man explained how Micah had made him his priest, upon which the Danites asked him to inquire of God if their journey would be prosperous. The priest, seemingly without hesitation, told the men to go on their way in peace and that the presence of the LORD would be with them.

What exactly was the mission of the five men? Sadly, the history of the tribe of Dan[11] is not good. Jacob, in his patriarchal blessing, makes a bleak prophecy, "Dan shall be a serpent by the way, a viper by the path, that bites the horse's heels, so that its rider shall fall backward" (Gen 49:17). Moses, in his tribal blessing, compares Dan to a lion, "Dan is a lion's whelp; he shall leap from Bashan" (Deut 33:22). The sad thing about the tribe of Dan is that they never fully possessed the inheritance that God had given them under Joshua. Their original land, bordering on Judah, Ephraim and Manasseh, stretched to the sea coast on the west, but Dan never managed to fully possess the lowland. The narrator informs us, "And the Amorites forced the children of Dan into the mountains, for they would not allow them to come down to the valley; and the Amorites were determined to dwell in Mount Heres, in Aijalon, and in Shaalbim; yet when the strength of the house of Joseph became greater, they were put under tribute" (1:34-35). Dan never managed to overcome the Amorites as Joseph was later able to do. They began to seek another area where they could resettle - hence the reason for the visit from the Danites.

The tribe of Dan had sent five of their men to seek and find a new inheritance. Having paused for a while in the mountains of Ephraim, they left the lodgings of Micah and travelled far north until they reached a town called Laish. The five Danites were delighted to discover a settlement that was isolated from other people. The inhabitants lived quiet unsuspecting lives, similar in many ways to the Sidonians. The five had found what they wanted and retraced their steps back to their brethren at Zorah and Eshtaol. On being asked for their report, the five gave an enthusiastic account of a large and fruitful land inhabited by a quiet and vulnerable people. They pressed on their brethren, "Arise, let us go up against them. For we have seen the land, and indeed it is very good. Would you do nothing? Do not hesitate to go and possess the land..." (18:9).

Six hundred men of Dan, armed for war, set out to go and take the new inheritance. They travelled through Judah and into the mountains of Ephraim, eventually arriving at the house of Micah. The original five spies informed their fellow tribesmen that in the houses of Micah there were household idols, carved and molten images, as well as an ephod. While the six hundred armed men waited at the gate, the five entered the house of Micah and lifted all the religious objects. On being challenged by the Levite, the five men told him to come with them to be a father and a priest to the tribe of Dan. What a career opportunity for the young man – from being a household priest to being a priest for a whole tribe! The young Levite found the offer to be irresistible, and took his place among the Danites. The company then turned to leave, putting the children and livestock in front.

On discovering what had happened, Micah mustered his neighbours and chased hard after the Danites until he caught up with them. When Micah called out, the Danites turned round and asked him why he had brought such a company with him. Exasperated, Micah protested that they had stolen his priest and his gods and yet they had the audacity to ask what ailed him! The Danites told him to be quiet lest some in their company should hear them and slay them. Micah knew that the Danites were too many and too strong for him and reluctantly turned for home.

The tribe of Dan had evidently felt the need for some kind of religion to validate their existence and underpin their future in a new land. Unfortunately, their concept of religion was totally removed from the revealed truth that God had given to Moses. They could have returned to the commandments and covenants of the living God, but instead invented their own religion. If it were a serious error for the people of Dan to mix truth with error, how much more for those today who, having the full revelation of God in the Bible, still regard religious blessing as something to be bought and sold.

The men of Dan continued on their journey until they reached Laish, where they burned the city with fire and slew all the inhabitants with the sword. We are told, "There was no deliverer, because it was far from Sidon, and they had no ties with anyone" (18:28). The question arises whether the slaughter of the people of Laish was within the original brief of God's command to Joshua to dispossess the Canaanites. It would appear that the move to Laish was not of God. In fact, the episode at the house of Micah demonstrated that the people of Dan had set themselves outside the will and purposes of God. They changed the name of Laish to Dan and set up the carved image that came from the house of Micah. Dan became a centre of idolatry and a place of stumbling for Israel until the day of the captivity of the land (18:30-31).

When we come to the New Testament, we discover that Dan is not included in the list of tribes comprising the one hundred and forty-four thousand as detailed in Revelation Chapter 7. Dan had chosen its idols in preference to the living God. Whether or not the name of Dan will be on the gates of the Holy City referred to in Revelation Chapter 21, is impossible to say.

The narrator, however, has kept the greatest shock of all to the end. The identity of the young Levite is now revealed – his name is Jonathan, the son of Gershom, the son of Moses![12] In other words, Jonathan was the grandson of Moses, no less. How staggering to consider what amount of truth can be lost within three generations. The religion of the people had become corrupt in the extreme.

This is a timely warning for our own generation. Professing Christian denominations are abandoning the truth of scripture and are adopting the prevailing ideas of a secular and increasingly hedonistic society. Further, we are being told that all religions are simply different expressions of one reality. In 2009 there was a meeting in Melbourne of the *The Parliament for World Religions*, the aim of which was the "strengthening of religious and spiritual communities by providing a special focus on indigenous and Aboriginal spiritualities; facilitating cooperation between Pagan, Jewish, Christian, Bahai, Jain, Muslim, Buddhist, Sikh and Hindu communities." The next meeting of the Parliament is to take place in Brussels in 2014.

The western governments are pushing a pluralistic agenda, giving 'equality laws' preference over religious freedom. How should the Bible believing Christian respond to such developments? The answer to this problem is obvious, even as it was in the days of Micah. Let us not make the mistake of the Danites. We must return to the teaching of the Bible without compromise, proclaiming Christ and Him crucified, while insisting on the uniqueness of His person and work.

---

[11] For a helpful history of the twelve tribes, see *The Names on the Gates of Pearl* by C.H. Waller, 1875 (Gospel Folio Press, Grand Rapids MI, republished 1997).
[12] It is overwhelmingly agreed among the commentators that 'Manasseh' should read 'Moses'. See, for example, page 184 of *Judges and Ruth* by Cundall and Morris (Tyndale Old Testament Commentaries, reprint 2008).

CHAPTER TWELVE

Judges 19:1 – 21:25

Descent into Hedonism

The final case study in the Book of Judges is shocking beyond words. Wrong doctrine inevitably leads to wrong behaviour. Paul tells us in his letter to the Romans that when men become foolish in their thinking, they consequently become perverse in their conduct. Their false worldview leads them to sexual behaviour of an unnatural, vile and unseemly kind (Rom 1:19-32). Hedonism, or the pursuit of pleasure, became the philosophy of life for fallen mankind. On reading the story of the Levite and his concubine, we become witnesses to a ghastly deed of violence carried out by men who had become amoral, having abandoned any attempt at self-control, allowing their passions to rule their behaviour.

A Levite from the mountains of Ephraim had taken a concubine from Bethlehem of Judah. The concubine was unfaithful to the Levite and played the harlot, eventually leaving him and returning to her father's house. After a period of four months, the man went after her and spoke kindly to her, asking her to come back with him. The man was welcomed by his father-in-law, who persuaded him to stay for three days. The narrator informs us, "Now his father-in-law, the young woman's father, detained him; and he stayed with him three days. So they ate and drank and lodged there" (19:4).

After a number of delays, the man finally left with his wife and servant and reached the city of Jebus as the day was drawing to a close. Jebus, later to be known as Jerusalem, was at that time still inhabited by Canaanites. The servant suggested that they lodge in Jebus, but the Levite did not want to spend the night in a city of foreigners. Instead, he preferred to keep travelling as far as Gibeah or Ramah where they would be safer among Israelites - or so he thought.

They arrived in the Benjamite city of Gibeah as the sun was going down. After some unsuccessful attempts to find lodging, the Levite decided to spend the night in the open square of the city. As they were settling down for their night's rest, an old man was returning home from his work in the fields. The man stopped and enquired of the company where they had come from and where they were going. As they conversed, they soon discovered that they had something in common – both the Levite and the old man came from the mountains of Ephraim. The man insisted that they should not stay in the open square, but rather lodge with him overnight. He took them to his home, gave fodder to the donkeys, and food and drink to his guests. They settled down to enjoy themselves, not realising the horror that lay ahead.

As they relaxed in pleasant conversation, their peace was disturbed by evil men who beat on the door of the house, demanding that the visitor be brought out. They said to the owner "Bring out the man who came into your house, that we may know him" (19:22 ESV). Their intention was to sodomise him. It was bad enough that the godless men of Sodom should descend to such conduct, but how much worse was it for the men of Benjamin to practise such perversion. They knew that God had called such activity an abomination (Lev 18:22).

Alarmingly, the twenty-first century is becoming more and more characterised by the sin of Sodom. One of the most abused words in the English language today is "homophobia". In the UK, people can now lose their livelihood by being labelled homophobic. Recent Equality laws in the UK are turning out to be anti-Christian. The Western world is currently pushing the 'gay' agenda and is trampling on those who take a Biblical view of homosexuality.

The old man pleaded with the men of Gibeah not to violate his guest. His suggestion at a compromise, however, was equally loathsome. He offered to let them have his own virgin daughter, along with the man's concubine, to humble and abuse. The men wouldn't agree until the Levite finally brought out his concubine and left her at their mercy. We read the horrendous words, "And they knew her and abused her all night until morning; and when the day began to break, they let her go" (19:25).

No one comes out of this story well. The men of Gibeah were guilty of violent and debased behaviour; the old man thought it more honourable to offer his virgin daughter than to have his guest defiled; the Levite's action was lamentable as he abandoned his concubine-wife to gang rape. The men abused the woman all night, eventually letting her go at day break. This was unrestrained sin by a society that had broken down, the end result of rebellion against God, the nadir of human behaviour. The people of Gibeah had lost sight of the sanctity of the human body as enshrined in the Law of Moses.

The morning scene makes painful reading, "When her master arose in the morning, and opened the doors of the house and went to go his way, there was his concubine, fallen at the door of the house, with her hands on the threshold" (19:27). Given that her master *arose* in the morning, we can assume that he had been lying down for his night's sleep. How horrible to think that while his concubine was being ravaged by pitiless men outside, he had been lying down taking his rest. Apparently, there was no one able or willing to save the woman's life.

The Levite, on opening the door and seeing his concubine lying on the ground, told the woman to get up. His callousness and lack of sympathy are staggering. When there was no answer, he lifted her on to the donkey and set off for his home. On arrival at his house, he took a knife and cut his concubine, limb by limb, into twelve pieces. The Levite then sent the twelve body pieces for viewing throughout the twelve tribes of Israel.

118

Those who saw the dismembered body limbs reacted with horror and indignation saying, "No such deed has been done or seen from the day that the children of Israel came up from the land of Egypt until this day. Consider it, confer, and speak up!" (19:30).

The nation had reached a defining moment in its history. What kind of community did they want to be? The people knew that something horrendous had been done among them. Should such behaviour go unpunished? In other words, how should they address the problem of guilt by their brethren?

Soon the people of Israel were travelling from all parts of the country to meet before the LORD at Mizpeh. They came from as far as Dan in the north, Beersheba in the south, and from Gilead across the Jordan. The leaders of the tribes presented themselves in the assembly together with forty thousand swordsmen. The Levite was asked to tell the gathered company what had actually happened. He recounted how the men of Gibeah had surrounded the house and had originally wanted to kill him, but how instead they had ravished his concubine all night until she died. The Levite ended his chilling account by challenging the people, "Look! All of you are children of Israel; give your advice and counsel here and now!" (20:7). The Levite did not describe how he had pushed the woman out of the house to the mercy of the men. He had retold the story so that nothing would reflect on him. He had been less than honest.

The people made a unanimous decision to go to Gibeah to repay it for all the vileness that had been committed by its inhabitants. The narrator tells us, "So all the men of Israel were gathered against the city, united together as one man" (20:11). The Israelites sent throughout the tribe of Benjamin an ultimatum, demanding that they deliver the guilty men of Gibeah so that they could be put to death. The men of Benjamin would not listen to the voice of their brethren the Israelites, and prepared themselves for war.

There was a considerable imbalance between the two

opposing armies. The swordsmen of Israel numbered four hundred thousand against the twenty-six thousand swordsmen of Benjamin, besides the seven hundred of Gibeah. Before attacking, the children of Israel went up to the house of God to enquire as to who should lead the attack against the people of Benjamin. The answer from the LORD was unambiguous - "Judah first!"

There is a sad parallel between the opening and closing stories of the book of Judges. The book opened with the tribe of Judah leading the fight against their enemies the Canaanites; the book closes with the tribe of Judah leading the fight against their brethren the Benjamites. What a commentary on human nature! As Christians, we should learn the lesson and make sure that we are not warring with our brethren.

The first two assaults on Gibeah met with ferocious resistance from the people of Benjamin. On the first occasion the Benjamites repulsed the attack by slaying twenty-two thousand Israelites. This prompted the Israelites to go up and weep before the LORD until evening, enquiring if they should again make battle with their brother Benjamin. The LORD's answer was to go up against them again. On the second occasion the Benjamites slew another eighteen thousand men, causing great searching of heart among the Israelites who went up to the house of God weeping. We read, "They sat there before the LORD and fasted that day until evening; and they offered burnt offerings and peace offerings before the LORD" (20:26). The narrator has inserted the parenthesis that in those days the ark of the covenant of God was in the care of Phinehas, the grandson of Aaron.

On the third day the Israelites prepared a battle strategy. The plan was to draw out the people of Benjamin from the town of Gibeah and then to encircle their army with men hidden in the fields. The Israelites approached Gibeah as they had done on the other two occasions and the people came out to engage them in battle, just as before. This time the Israelites deliberately retreated, drawing the Benjamites far enough out of the city to cut off their retreat, at which moment those waiting in ambush entered the city and set it on fire. The rising smoke was the signal for the retreating Israelites to turn around and attack the Benjamites, while at the same time the Israelites came out of the city, entrapping and encircling them. The Benjamites, totally enveloped, were heavily defeated that day, losing twenty-five thousand swordsmen against Israel's much smaller loss of thirty men.

In the days following, the Israelites went on a rampage of destruction through the cities of Benjamin, setting them on fire and killing any men or animals they happened to find. The only male survivors of Benjamin were six hundred swordsmen who fled from the fighting at Gibeah to the rock of Rimmon, staying there for four months. The tribe of Benjamin had nearly been wiped out in this fratricidal war.

The punishment on Benjamin was, on the face of it, very extreme. The slaying of twenty five thousand men as a punishment for what was done by a small number of men does seem to be disproportionate. It is true that sin must be dealt with, but it is also true that we should first examine ourselves to make sure that we are not removing a speck from our brother's eye when we ought to be removing the plank from our own eye (Mat 7:3-4).

In times of anger or stress we often make vows which we later come to regret. We have already observed how Jephthah bitterly regretted his foolish vow. We now learn that the Israelites, in their anger, had made a vow concerning Benjamin, saying "None of us shall give his daughter to Benjamin as a wife" (21:1). The Israelites were soon to regret this rash oath. The tribe of Benjamin had been decimated and now the problem for the Israelites was how to save it from extinction. If the few remaining survivors were not allowed to take wives from the women of Israel, the tribe would soon cease to exist.

The children of Israel returned again to the house of God, weeping bitterly and complaining about their predicament, "O

Lord God of Israel, why has this come to pass in Israel, that today there should be one tribe missing in Israel?" (21:3). The next day they built an altar and offered burnt offerings and peace offerings. We do not read that the LORD gave them any answer. The leaders devised a rather disingenuous plan to circumvent their vow. They made enquiries as to who had not come up to Mizpah with the assembly to the LORD, for they had made yet another vow concerning such men, "He shall surely be put to death" (21:5). After some investigation, it was discovered that no one from the city of Jabesh Gilead had come to Mizpah. The congregation then sent twelve thousand armed men on a mission to Jabesh Gilead to kill all the men and women and to spare only the young virgins. They carried out their grisly task with zeal, destroying every man and woman, and sparing only four hundred young virgins which they brought to Shiloh.

The Israelites sent words of peace to the men of Benjamin who were at the rock of Rimmon, telling them to come and take wives of the four hundred virgins who had been spared from the destruction of Jabesh Gilead. The problem, however, was that there were still not enough partners for all six hundred Benjamites. And so another plan was hatched to secure wives for the remaining two hundred men, without breaking the conditions of the original vow. The Israelites told the men of Benjamin that there would soon be a yearly feast of the LORD at Shiloh, and that they should hide in the vineyards until the daughters of Shiloh came out to perform their dances. At that moment, each man was to catch a wife for himself. If there were any objections from fathers or brothers, they were to be given this explanation, "Be kind to them for our sakes, because we did not take a wife for any of them in the war; for it is not as though you have given the women to them at this time, making yourselves guilty of your oath" (21:22).

The narrator informs us that the children of Benjamin did so, catching wives from the women of Shiloh and returning with them to their inheritance in the land of Benjamin. They rebuilt their cities and dwelt in them. When the matter of Benjamin was finally considered closed, the other tribes also returned to their own homes, families, and inheritance. And so the book of Judges closes with the significant observation, "In those days there was no king in Israel; everyone did what was right in his own eyes" (21:25).

The problems within Israel were entirely of their own making. They made rash vows when they were angry, with disastrous consequences. This would remind us of King Herod who made a rash vow when he was intoxicated and excited (Matt 14:6-11). Later he bitterly regretted having made the oath. There is an important lesson for Christians to learn from these incidents, and that is to practise self-control. A man is at his most vulnerable when he is consumed with anger, or lust, or under the influence of alcohol. These are all described by Paul in the New Testament as the works of the flesh,

"Now the works of the flesh are evident, which are: adultery, fornication, uncleanness, lewdness, idolatry, sorcery, hatred, contentions, jealousies, ambitions, dissensions, heresies, envy, murders, drunkenness, revelries, and the like; of which I tell you beforehand, just as I also told you in time past, that those who practise such things will not inherit the kingdom of God" (Galatians 5:19-21).

By contrast, Paul also speaks of the fruit of the Spirit, "But the fruit of the Spirit is love, joy, peace, longsuffering, kindness, goodness, faithfulness, gentleness, self-control" (Galatians 5:22-23).

Christians should be known for their moderation. The overseers in a local church should apply discipline with wisdom, grace and love. Assembly discipline on a brother should be with a view to his restoration, not his destruction. The elders responsible for such discipline should avoid rash oaths. The same lesson applies to the individual member of the local assembly. He or she should avoid rash oaths or threats when they are angry. Problems between brethren can sometimes persist for years because someone swears they will never be reconciled unless such and such a thing happens first. They put themselves on a hook and have great difficulty getting off. That is exactly what the Israelites did in the matter of Benjamin. The punishment was extreme and the vows were unwise. The last story of the book of Judges is a warning against treating fellow Christians rashly, as if they were our enemies rather than our brethren.

CHAPTER THIRTEEN

No King in Israel

The book of Judges has certainly been a strange mixture of the good, the bad and the ugly. Is there a plan to the book or is it just a random compilation of unconnected stories?[13] The following observations show clearly that there is a discernable structure and thought flow in the order of the narratives.

The book begins with two introductions and closes with two epilogues. In between we have seven stories of major captivities and deliverers. At the beginning of the book, the people are fighting their enemies the Canaanites; at the end of the book, the people are fighting with their brethren the Benjamites. At the beginning of the book, the people are practising intermittent idolatry; at the end of the book, idolatry has been institutionalised.

Between the beginning and the end of the book a great deterioration has taken place. What was the turning point? The answer to this question is found in the central story of Gideon. Before the time of Gideon, the people were fighting their enemies; after Gideon, the people were fighting their brethren. The failure to make a distinction between one's enemies and one's friends becomes a significant problem after Gideon. Before Gideon, Othniel married a believing Hebrew woman and she became the secret of his success; after Gideon, Samson married unconverted Philistine women who contributed to his failure. Before Gideon, Ehud slew the Moabite enemies at the fords of Jordan; after Gideon, Jephthah slew his Ephraimite brethren at the fords of Jordan. Before Gideon, Jael pierced the skull of Sisera the Canaanite; after

Gideon, the woman of Thebez crushed the skull of Abimelech the son of Gideon.

The turning-point began when Gideon flailed the men of Succoth with thorns, and went on to tear down the tower of Penuel, killing the men of the city who were his fellow Israelites. Gideon had set a terrible precedent which would be followed for years to come.

Unity of brethren

A major theme in the book of Judges is the treatment of our brethren. How easy it is to take our eyes off the Lord and to cast them critically on fellow believers. The church of God at Corinth was plagued with such problems. Paul wrote, "For where there are envy, strife, and divisions among you, are you not carnal and behaving like mere men?" (1 Cor 3:3). Divisions in a local church will spoil both worship and gospel witness. Instead of taking the gospel out to the world, energy is wasted with infighting and strife.

The problems among brethren are often not doctrinal but personal. This seems to have been the case at Philippi where two sisters had fallen out. Such a scenario can affect the whole assembly. Paul made an appeal to both women to be at peace, "I implore Euodia and I implore Syntyche to be of the same mind in the Lord" – and in case the two ladies needed help to be reconciled – "And I urge you also, true companion, help these women..." (Phil 4:2-3). We do not know who the companion or yokefellow was, but obviously he was a brother whom Paul considered to be capable of mediation and peacemaking. It is a function of the elders to watch over their flock and to act when they see a contention arising. Every assembly of believers needs a watchful and helpful "yokefellow".

Not all church problems however, are caused by personality clashes. The divisions can also relate to church doctrine and practice. In such cases, the elders must discern between things that are essential and things that are non-essential. If the issues in contention are essential doctrine, such as the virgin birth or deity of Christ, then there must be total unity. There can be no compromise on things which are essential.

Some divisive issues, however, which are purported to be doctrinal, are often about non-essential things. In such cases, the principle of liberty becomes operative. That is the teaching of Romans Chapter 14. Paul advises us that such things as abstinence from meat and the esteeming of certain days are examples of non-essential things on which there can be compromise. But the exercise of our liberty must be moderated by consideration for the weaker brother. In other words, if my insistence on my liberty will stumble a weaker brother, I should forego my liberty. Richard Baxter, the English Puritan, is credited with this beautiful summary, "Unity in things which are essential; liberty in things which are not essential; and charity in all".

Very often, the differences which tear assemblies apart are about non-essential issues which could and should be resolved in the spirit of Romans Chapter 14. The same principles which govern relations within an assembly, should also govern relations between assemblies. Paul writes, "Therefore let us pursue the things which make for peace and the things by which one may edify another" (Rom 14:19). Let us learn the lesson from the book of Judges - we must not slay our brethren because they pronounce 'shibboleth' differently.

Restoration

The patience and kindness of God is a leading theme in the book of Judges. Great encouragement and comfort can be drawn from the book for those who have fallen back and lost ground in their Christian journey.

Throughout the book, there is a repeating cycle of disobedience and captivity, followed by repentance and deliverance. We read before each of the captivities that "the children of Israel again did that which was evil in the sight of the LORD". As a result the LORD delivered them into the power of their enemies until life became intolerable and they cried to the LORD for deliverance. The incredible truth is that in each case the LORD heard them and sent them a deliverer. The duration of the deliverance was usually between forty and eighty years. After Othniel, the land had rest forty years; after Ehud, eighty years; after Deborah and Barak, forty years; in the days of Gideon, forty years. But in each case, the people invariably reverted to idolatry, and God would once again chastise and deliver them.

We are left wondering why God should bother with such an unfaithful people. The answer must surely be found in the character of God. He loved Israel, and delighted to forgive and bless. God had gracious purposes for them in keeping with His promises to Abraham. Like the father running to meet the returning prodigal, God always welcomed repentance and faith on the part of His people. After all, He is the God who says that a man should forgive a repentant offender seventy times seven.

This is good news for the Christian who has experienced defeat in his or her life. The Lord Jesus forgives and restores. When we are weary with our journey, He is our Great High Priest; and if we sin, He is our Advocate with the Father. How thankful we should be that God is forgiving, patient, loving and kind. The book of Judges has much to teach on the beautiful theme of restoration. Remember that Samson's hair began to grow again.

Lessons in Christian Warfare

We have learnt many lessons about warfare in our reading of the book of Judges. We noted at the beginning of this book that Israel's enemies were real 'flesh and blood' people who fought with literal material weapons of war. This is not the case for the Christian, and yet each of Israel's enemies becomes a powerful symbol of the dangers which the modern Christian must face. For example, the Mesopotamians speak of *friendship and love of the world;* Moab speaks of *the flesh;* the Gentile

Canaanites symbolise *the wisdom of this world;* Midian means *strife;* Ammon is that aspect of *the world which would rob us of our inheritance;* the Philistines, who are continually referred to as 'uncircumcised', speak of *the world's religions as false, unclean, and alienated from God.*

With this formidable array of enemies, how can the Christian withstand the attacks? The most detailed combat manual for the Christian is to be found in Ephesians Chapter 6. Interestingly, there is only one offensive weapon allowed – everything else is for defence. The first part of the Christian's kit is truth. The devil is the father of lies and will always attack the truth. Our waist is to be girded with truth. Second, we are to put on the breastplate of righteousness. If there is unrighteousness in our lives, the devil will use it to destroy our testimony. The third item concerns our footwear. Our feet are to be shod with the preparation of the gospel of peace. Feet are used for walking, and there is obviously the idea of moving out with the message of peace and life. Fourth, we are to take the shield of faith for defence against the devil's burning arrows. When we are under satanic attack, it is our faith which will grasp that there is victory out ahead, and our faith which will see Him who is invisible. Fifth, we are to wear the helmet of salvation. This is to protect our minds. Sixth, the Christian is to take the only offensive weapon mentioned - a sword. It is not a metal sword, however, but the sword of the Spirit which is the word of God. We must read and familiarise ourselves with the scriptures. And lastly, we are to pray in the Spirit. Prayer **is** the vital lifeline and link with God. Paul tells us to put on the whole armour of God that we might be able to stand against the wiles of the devil. God gives us all the resources we need to live a victorious Christian life until our last day on earth.

No King in Israel

We are told four times in the book of Judges that, "In those days there was no king in Israel" (17:6; 18:1; 19:1; and 21:25). In two of these references we are given the additional information that, "everyone did what was right in his own eyes"(17:6; 21:25).

When we read the stories of idolatry, murder and sexual violence we might well wonder if there were any godly people left in Israel. How refreshing, therefore, when we come to the book of Ruth to read about a man called Boaz. Happily, there were still godly men and women in the land of Israel, even in the days of the Judges!

Samuel the prophet anointed Saul the Benjamite as Israel's first king. After Saul lost the kingdom because of disobedience, Samuel then anointed David of the tribe of Judah as the new king, a man after God's own heart. David's successors included both good kings and bad kings up until the last reigning monarch, Zedekiah, who was taken to Babylon by Nebuchadnezzar. The line of descent, however, continued right up to the birth of our Lord Jesus Christ at Bethlehem. Into this world came a greater than Solomon and a greater than Jonah. He was even greater than the very temple in Jerusalem.

The angel Gabriel spoke to Mary concerning her first-born Son,

"Do not be afraid, Mary, for you have found favour with God. And behold, you will conceive in your womb and bring forth a Son, and shall call His name JESUS. He will be great, and will be called the Son of the Highest; and the Lord God will give Him the throne of His father David. And He will reign over the house of Jacob forever, and of His kingdom there will be no end" (Luke 1:30-33).

Later, when Jesus had been born, wise men from the East arrived at Jerusalem enquiring about the whereabouts of the newborn King,

"Where is He who has been born King of the Jews? For we have seen His star in the East and have come to worship Him" (Matt 2:2).

The Lord Jesus had not come to set up His Kingdom at that time, but to deal with the great problem of sin and evil. For about thirty-three years, the Lord lived a holy and sinless life in the nation of Israel. Their King was living among them but they did not know Him. The rulers of the nation eventually handed Jesus of Nazareth over to the Roman authorities for crucifixion. Pilate challenged the Jews, "Shall I crucify your King?" The chief priests gave their notorious answer, "We have no king but Caesar!" Pilate conceded and delivered the Lord Jesus to be crucified on a cross between two criminals. A title was written and put on the cross,

JESUS OF NAZARETH, THE KING OF THE JEWS

After suffering for six hours on the cross, the Lord Jesus proclaimed, "It is finished" (John 19:30) and bowing His head, dismissed His spirit. The sin question had been settled forever – God could now forgive men their sins on righteous grounds. Christ's suffering for sin will never be repeated. He rose from the dead and sat down at God's right hand in heaven. But, we might well ask, what about His kingdom? This is a good question and was asked by the disciples before He ascended to heaven, "Lord, will you at this time restore the kingdom to Israel?" (Acts 1:6). The Lord Jesus replied that they were not privy to God's programme which He would carry out in His own time. Their commission was to be witnesses unto the Lord Jesus Christ in Jerusalem, Judea, Samaria and then all the earth. God's only message for the world today is the gospel concerning His Son.

In this present age or dispensation of grace, God makes no difference between the Jew and the Gentile. All are sinners and all must come the same way: by repentance toward God and faith in the Lord Jesus Christ.

Does that mean that the kingdom of Israel is finished forever and is now to be understood in spiritual terms only (amillennialism). We contend that such a view is seriously in error and does not do justice to the many Old Testament texts which attest to future glory and blessing for Israel. We quote some prophecies to show that there will again be a King in Israel,

> "Lift up your heads, O you gates!
> Lift up, you everlasting doors!
> And the King of glory shall come in.
> Who is this King of glory?
> The Lord of hosts,
> He is the King of glory."

Psalm 24:9-10

This Psalm speaks of the glorious moment when the Lord Jesus will return and enter Jerusalem. Zechariah also speaks of the same event,

> "For I will gather all the nations to battle against Jerusalem...Then the LORD will go forth and fight against those nations, And in that day His feet will stand on the Mount of Olives...
> And the LORD shall be King over all the earth.
> In that day it shall be – "The LORD is one," and His name one."

Zechariah 14:2,3,4,9.

Isaiah also tells us about a future King,

> "Behold, a king will reign in righteousness, and princes will rule with justice"

Isaiah 32:1

The Lord Jesus also spoke of the future day when He would come to Jerusalem and gather the believing remnant of Israel,

"Immediately after the tribulation of those days the sun will be darkened, and the moon will not give its light; the stars will fall from heaven, and the powers of the heaven will be shaken. Then the sign of the Son of Man will appear in heaven, and then all the tribes of the earth will mourn, and they will see the

Son of Man coming on the clouds of heaven with power and great glory. And He will send His angels with a great sound of a trumpet, and they will gather together His elect from the four winds, from one end of heaven to the other." Mat 24:29-31

These scriptures make it plain that the Lord Jesus will return to reign on earth. The first time He came it was to deal with sin; the second time He will come in power and great glory to judge and to reign.

The book of Judges ends on the mournful note that there was no king in Israel and that everyone did what was right in his own eyes. One day soon the rejected King will return to Israel and will reign in righteousness. All history is leading up to the glorious second advent of our Lord Jesus Christ, the King of Glory.

Conclusion

We have seen that the book of Judges has much to teach about the treatment of our brethren, the restoration of the erring believer, Christian warfare, and the coming King . There are lessons for individual Christians, for Christian leaders, and for local churches/assemblies. Finally, there are weighty lessons for governments and those in authority. When a nation's legislative body begins to abandon Bible-based morality in the areas of family, marriage and sexuality, moral chaos will follow. Western governments are currently de-Christianising existing laws under the pretext that they are out of place in new multi-faith pluralist societies. Ironically, the implications for religious freedom are alarming. The words of warning from Deborah echo down the millennia to our own day:

They chose new gods;
Then there was war in the gates

Song of Deborah, Judges 5:8

There will be a high price to pay when a nation chooses darkness rather than light. Sooner or later, to borrow wisdom from Deborah, there will be "war in the gates". As the foundations of a society are dismantled, that society will suffer greatly in the disintegration of the social and moral well-being of the nation.

What are individual Christians to do in a secularised anti-Christian society? We are surely to live as men and women of faith and follow the examples of the thirteen judges - Othniel, Ehud, Shamgar, Deborah, Barak, Gideon, Tola, Jair, Jephthah, Ibzan, Elon, Abdon and Samson. Let us live godly, separated lives unto our Lord Jesus Christ, bearing witness to Him in a Christ rejecting world. Let us return to the scriptures in humility and sincerity. We give the last word to Deborah:

My heart is with the rulers of Israel
Who offered themselves willingly with the people.
Bless the LORD!

Song of Deborah, Judges 5:9

---

[13] This question was clearly answered for me at a seminar conducted by Dr David Gooding in Apsley Hall, Belfast, back in February 2000. I am indebted to Dr Gooding for his observations on the thought flow of the book - see Table p.135.

TABLE OF CONTENTS OF THE BOOK OF JUDGES

THE MAJOR CAPTIVITIES AND DELIVERERS

1:1 - 3:6   17:1 - 21:25

TWO INTRODUCTIONS	6. GIDEON Enemy: Midian Tactic: Light in Earthen Vessels		TWO EPILOGUES
	↑	↓	
1. AFTER THE DEATH OF JOSHUA... *Who shall go up first against the Canaanites?* Covenant Bochim Weeping ↓	5. DEBORAH, BARAK, JAEL Enemy: Canaanites Tactic: Skull pierced with tent-peg ↑	7. WOMAN OF THEBEZ Enemy: Abimelech Tactic: Skull crushed with mill-stone ↓	11. BENJAMIN'S IMMORALITY *Who shall go up first against Benjamin?* Bethel Weeping Ark of Covenant ↑
2. WHEN JOSHUA HAD SENT THE PEOPLE AWAY Intermittent Idolatry ➡	4. EHUD Enemy: Moabites Tactic: Killing the enemy at the fords ↑	8. JEPHTHAH Enemy: Ammonites Tactic: Killing one's brethren (!) at the fords ↓	10. MICAH'S IDOLATRY Institutionalised Idolatry ↑
	3. OTHNIEL Enemy: Mesopotamians Secret of success: his wife	9. SAMSON Enemy: Philistines Secret of failure: his wives ➡	

Courtesy of Dr David Gooding

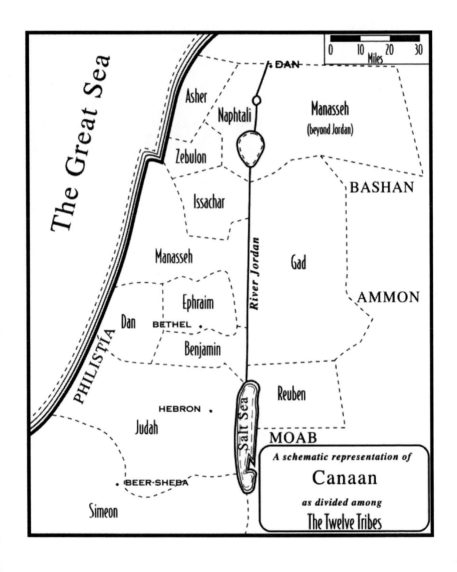

A schematic representation of
Canaan
as divided among
The Twelve Tribes

Select Bibliography

Cundall, Arthur E. and Morris, Leon *Judges and Ruth* (Tyndale Old Testament Commentaries Volume 7, Inter-Varsity Press, England, 1968)

Gooding, A.M.S. *The 13 Judges* (Gospel Tract Publications, Glasgow, 1986)

Hamlin, E. John *Judges: At Risk in the Promised Land* (International Theological Commentary, William B. Eerdmans Publishing Co, Grand Rapids, 1990)

Hercus, John *God is God: Samson and other case histories from the Book of Judges* (Hodder and Stoughton Limited, London, 1971)

Herzog, Chaim and Gichon, Mordechai "The Wars of the Judges" in *Battles of the Bible* (Greenhill Books, London, 2nd Edition 1997, first published 1978)

Kelly, William "Judges" in *The Earlier Historical Books of the Old Testament* (Central Bible Hammond Trust Ltd, Northumberland, modern reprint, first published 1874)

Lacey, C.T. *Judges* (What the Bible Teaches, Ritchie Old Testament Commentaries, John Ritchie Ltd, Kilmarnock, 2006)

Lockyer, Herbert *All the Men of the Bible* (Zondervan, Grand Rapids, modern reprint, first published 1958

Lockyer, Herbert *All the Women of the Bible* (Zondervan, Grand Rapids, modern reprint 1967)

Spilsbury, Julian "Mount Tabor" in *Great Military Disasters* (Quercus Books, London, 2010)

Stanton, Phil *Samson: The Secret of Strength* (Kingsway Publications, Eastbourne, 1996)

Waller, C.H. *The Names on the Gates of Pearl* (Gospel Folio Press, MI, reprint 1997, originally published 1875)

Wiersbe, Warren W. *Be Available: Judges* (Scripture Press, England, 1994)

Wilcock, Michael *The Message of Judges* (The Bible Speaks Today, Inter-Varsity Press, Nottingham, 1992)